PSYCHOANALYTIC ASPECTS OF FIELDWORK

JENNIFER C. HUNT

Qualitative Research Methods
Volume 18

SAGE PUBLICATIONS
The Publishers of Professional Social Science
Newbury Park   London   New Delhi

For my mother and father

For information address:

SAGE Publications, Inc.
2111 West Hillcrest Drive
Newbury Park, California 91320

SAGE Publications Ltd.
28 Banner Street
London EC1Y 8QE
England

SAGE Publications India Pvt. Ltd.
M-32 Market
Greater Kailash I
New Delhi 110 048 India

Library of Congress Cataloging-in-Publication Data

Hunt, Jennifer C.
    Psychoanalytic aspects of fieldwork / by Jennifer C. Hunt.
        p.   cm. — (Qualitative research methods ; v. 18)
    Bibliography: p.
    ISBN 0-8039-3472-6. — ISBN 0-8039-3473-4 (pbk.)
    1. Sociology — Field work — Psychological aspects. 2. Participant observation — Psychological aspects. 3. Sociologists — Psychology.
    I. Title. II. Series.
  HM24.H875   1989
301′.0723 — dc20   89-35855
                                                              CIP

FIRST PRINTING, 1989

When citing a University Paper, please use the proper form. Remember to cite the correct Sage University Paper series title and include the paper number. One of the following formats can be adapted (depending on the style manual used):

(1) KIRK, JEROME and MARC L. MILLER (1986) Reliability and Validity in Qualitative Research. Sage University Paper Series on Qualitative Research Methods, Vol. 1. Beverly Hills, CA: Sage.

or

(2) Kirk, J., & Miller, M. L. (1986). *Reliability and validity in qualitative research* (Sage University Paper Series on Qualitative Research Methods, Vol. 1). Beverly Hills, CA: Sage.

CONTENTS

EDITORS' INTRODUCTION

The literature on fieldwork and field methods is redolent with echoes. The first kind of echo is the echo of the experience in the field as written in publications and research reports. These are often found summarized in publications in "methods sections." The second is the echo of one's fieldwork in one's personal life and career and the investment of the field self in one's subsequent research and writing. These echoes are found written in autobiographies and biographies and essays about how one's fieldwork or relations with informants have changed one's life. A less commonly explored echo is that of one's own past as reflected in one's choice of research problem, method, setting, and even informants in the field. These echoes are less likely to be written about, although they are a part of the oral tradition of fieldwork. A part of the context, a fundamental part indeed of the context of fieldwork, is the presence of images, beliefs, feelings, and memories that are not directly stimulated by conscious knowledge of the here and now. Fieldworkers, like the rest of us, are variously elsewhere and with people other than those encountered. These sorts of echoes are well explored in Jennifer Hunt's book, the 18th Volume in the Sage Series on Qualitative Methods.

Since the self is the key fieldwork tool, the role of self-understanding is critical to well executed fieldwork. Jennifer Hunt argues here, in a unique attempt to integrate social science and psychoanalytic thinking, that a central concern of fieldwork methods should be exploring the relationships between subject, researcher, and data and the unconscious seen in intrapsychic conflicts. She draws on the tradition of anthropology that resonates with the work of the psychoanalytically oriented and which urges researchers to explore how their own conflicts and unconscious, called by some "transference," might affect their research. Hunt suggests that the analogue of transference phenomena can be found in fieldwork. This is a bold effort that requires honesty and forthrightness. She uses the notion of transference broadly, examining how psychic conflicts are revealed in the field and how the individual's past shapes present understandings. She makes the case, using the work of other social science researchers as well as her own work on policing, that an

5

understanding of the fundamental grounding of experience in the past, a psychosocially constructed and shaped past, is essential. Because she has been so honest about her own learning process, she makes an important contribution to the fieldwork tradition.

This book, which some may call an attempt to be heard across disciplinary chasms, raises very basic questions about the way in which echoes, both soft and loud, pattern our sensibilities. Furthermore, Hunt raises fundamental questions about such continuing issues as "going native," "validity," and reliability of field data. She continues the ongoing dialogue in this series concerning the role of field data in shaping social science methods and theory.

—John Van Maanen
Peter K. Manning
Marc L. Miller

ACKNOWLEDGMENTS

I am grateful to a number of friends and colleagues for their help during various stages in the formulation and writing of this monograph. Bryce Boyer, Shula Reinharz, Barbara Hogan, Ruth Horowitz, Steve Leinen, Caryl Oris, and Alison Orr-Andrawes all provided encouragement. Daniel Papernik and Stephen K. Firestein shared their understanding of the clinical narrative and encouraged me to find the poetry that lay between the lines. John Van Maanen, in his humorous and tactful way, provided helpful comments. I owe a special debt to Marie Rudden who lent her kind and critical eye to several drafts of this manuscript. Finally, I thank my friend and colleague Peter K. Manning for his patience, support, and faith in me. The writing of some parts of this manuscript was facilitated by an SBR grant awarded by Montclair State College.

PSYCHOANALYTIC ASPECTS OF FIELDWORK

JENNIFER C. HUNT

1. INTRODUCTION

This book examines the methodological implications of a psychoanalytic perspective for sociological fieldwork. Psychoanalysis is the study of intrapsychic conflict and unconscious mental life. The psychoanalytic exploration of fieldwork pays particular attention to the psychodynamic dimension of the research encounter and how unconscious processes structure relations between researcher, subject, and the data gathered. The psychoanalytic framework utilized here is derived from the theoretical and methodological works of Sigmund Freud. There are a number of concepts which are fundamental to the classical psychoanalytic tradition. These will be examined in relevant chapters of this monograph.

Chapter 1 includes a general discussion of fieldwork and the dominant sociological approaches to its study. Particular attention is paid to how different schools view researcher subjectivity, the role played by affective and cognitive processes in research, and the definition of the researcher as a person and investigative tool. Some of these issues relate to epistemological assumptions about the relationship between researcher and subjects and the nature of reality.

Chapter 2 defines psychoanalytic theory and method and shows how these differ from traditional sociological approaches to fieldwork. Subsequent chapters attempt to apply the psychoanalytic perspective to the fieldwork process. Emphasis is placed on those dimensions of the fieldwork encounter which promote intrapsychic conflict and transference reactions in the researcher. The experience of culture shock, the assumption of certain fieldwork roles, and the unconscious meaning of the investigative process are explored. A section on transference and countertransference in clinical and fieldwork settings uses case studies to examine the unconscious structuring of research relations and data gathering. The book concludes with a brief discussion of some practical problems of doing applied psychoanalysis.

Some data used in this study were borrowed from the published literature on fieldwork. Other materials were gleaned from fieldnotes collected during eighteen months of research in the Metro City Police Department. In addition, interviews were conducted with researchers currently involved in fieldwork in both cross-cultural and native settings. The names of those researchers and some details of their experience are omitted from this account to protect the privacy of the people involved.

A word of caution is in order. The data utilized from fieldnotes and most published accounts of fieldwork were not gathered with the intention to do a psychoanalytic exploration. In fact, few sociologists have collected the kinds of materials which would facilitate an in-depth study of the psychodynamics of fieldwork and data collection. As a result, there are inevitable limitations in this research, and it is necessarily speculative in parts. It is hoped, however, that such an exploratory work will inspire other researchers to use their skills and creative imaginations to collect the kind of data which will facilitate the writing of more sophisticated studies of the fieldwork process which utilize both sociological and psychoanalytic insights.

Sociologists share with psychoanalysts an interest in exploring implicit meanings. Nevertheless, questions of the scientific validity of psychoanalytic theory and method may present a problem to those sociologists unfamiliar with clinical psychoanalysis and its mode of interpretive thinking. There is a rich literature on science and psychoanalysis that the skeptic might enjoy reviewing (e.g. Edelson, 1984; Hook, 1959). For my own part, I share with Robert Stoller (1983, p. 9) a disinterest in the subject and prefer to get on with the interpretive task, leaving others to debate its scientific status. It should be noted that this book does not offer a challenge to traditional sociological approaches to fieldwork. In contrast, it attempts to explore a domain of research relations that has been omitted from traditional discussions, in order to provide a complementary framework which will add depth and richness to the complex analysis of people studying people in social context.

The Fieldwork Endeavor

Fieldwork is a method of gathering in-depth data about the meaning structures, moral codes, and social behaviors of particular cultural groups and the individuals who compose their membership. It is characterized by intensive interaction between researcher and subjects. Typically, researchers immerse themselves in the subjects' natural setting for months or even years at a time. It is believed that an in-depth understanding of the rich texture of meaning can only be accomplished through such long-term, daily interaction.

Definitions of the subjects' meaning structures, i.e. the desired cultural data, vary depending on the theoretical and substantive concerns of the researcher. Traditionally, sociologists have restricted the definition of meaning to cultural phenomena, such as norms and values, and focused on data relevant to the interactional, political, and economic spheres of everyday life. Some sociologists have begun to collect data regarding people's emotional lives in order to explore the link between affects and interaction (Clark, 1987; Hochschild, 1983). In contrast, psychoanalytic anthropologists have defined their object of study more broadly. For example, they have routinely collected data on individuals' dreams, fantasies, and "parapraxes" (blunders such as slips of the tongue or pen or lapses in memory) in order to examine the unconscious dimensions of experience (Boyer, 1979; Gregor, 1985; Kracke, 1978; Obeyesekere, 1981; Kilborne, 1981).

Sociological data are gathered primarily through direct participation in the lives of subjects. Researchers assume different social roles and engage in a variety of group activities. Some roles are strategically planned by the researchers and take account of their knowledge of the complexities of culture. Others are invented on the spot, constituting creative responses to unanticipated situational events (Wax, 1983; Punch, 1986; Hunt, 1984). Most of the fieldworker's role-related actions involve behaviors which are peripheral to those of subjects but are, nevertheless, significant. For example, in fieldwork among urban police, gifts of "bourbon balls" (cookies) and a rum-flavored mango took on special cultural meaning (Hunt, 1984). Although I did not actually drink on duty with police, these gestures symbolized willingness to accept uncritically their routine involvement in these activities. As a result, police drank freely in my presence and ceased to conceal their engagement in certain other activities which violated departmental rules. Ultimately, my engagement in these kinds of symbolic behaviors facilitated access to the police officers' informal world of "normal force," lying, and corruption (Hunt, 1985; Hunt and Manning, in press).

Occasionally, researchers also participate directly in the social practices of subjects or engage in activities crucial to their lives. On one occasion, assistance was given to a police partner in subduing suspects during a knife fight in which several persons were critically wounded (Hunt, 1984, p. 290). During their fieldwork among high-level drug dealers, Peter and Patti Adler accompanied subjects on smuggling trips, attended parties, occasionally loaned money, and even provided their home as a place from which to conduct drug transactions (Adler and Adler, 1987; Adler, 1985). Obviously, there is much variation in the kinds of behaviors in which fieldworkers engage, depending on the demands of the setting, the methodological perspectives of the researchers, and their personal proclivities, ethics, and research goals.

Sociological fieldwork data is also gathered through direct observation of people in their natural settings. Extensive observations of everyday life provide a social context in which the researcher can determine the constitution of routine activity. They provide an important background which facilitates the interpretation of interview data by distinguishing social from individual behavioral patterns. Observations are also useful in gathering information about aspects of the social world in which the researcher hesitates to participate. In some instances, even observations may become personally problematic, and data are sacrificed. For example, in several instances during which police beat suspects, I left the scene. This action was not offensive to members because it indicated less moral antipathy than willingness to avoid the possible legal problems involved in becoming a witness. Devereux (1967) reports a similar reaction to a pig-killing ritual among a primitive group he studied. Indeed, he found their mode of slaughter so loathsome that he intervened and encouraged the use of more humane killing techniques.

In some situations, observational and participatory roles overlap in ways which facilitate research and minimize the fieldworker's personal discomfort. Laud Humphreys (1970) provides an interesting case in point in his discussion of the tearoom trade. Humphreys conducted fieldwork among homosexuals engaging in impersonal sex in public bathrooms. He avoided direct participation in gay mens' sexual activities while gathering detailed data. Thus, his observer status fit neatly in the "watch queen" role, which combined voyeuristic sexuality with being the lookout for other participants. In this unusual role of observer and participant, Humphreys resembled the dreamer who is both audience and actor in his nighttime play.

Fieldworkers may supplement participant observation with additional methodological techniques, including informal and formal interviewing and the recording of life histories. Document analysis and various "nonreactive" measures may also be employed (e.g. Webb et al., 1966; Denzin, 1970). Some researchers utilize a variety of instruments including coded questionnaires, video equipment, and tape recorders. In general, however, these devices are employed only after the researcher has spent some time in the field. The initial period of participant observation allows for the development of sufficient rapport with subjects to ensure their trust and cooperation. It also ensures that researchers are familiar enough with the world of research to formulate culturally relevant questions based on their understanding of native meaning structures rather than a priori assumptions (Schatzman and Strauss, 1967; Denzin, 1970).

Three essential features of fieldwork can be gleaned from this discussion. First, in contrast to scientific enterprises which rely largely on quantitative techniques and formal devices to study human and nonhuman phenomena, the researcher's self is the primary instrument of inquiry. Any mechanical device utilized in fieldwork is mediated through the researcher's own person and the kind of relationship he or she develops with subjects. Second, fieldwork is action rather than armchair research. It involves active participation in the subjects' lives as well as naturalistic observation. The degree of researcher participation deemed essential to gather data has been the subject of debate among sociological researchers. Nevertheless, this special stress on action and real-life involvement distinguishes fieldwork from other scientific enterprises, including laboratory research, quantitative data collecting in social science, and clinical psychoanalysis. Third, fieldwork involves a process of learning or secondary socialization in which researchers become sufficiently acquainted with the world of subjects to understand their modes of discourse, communicate in their language, and demonstrate culturally appropriate behaviors. However, the researchers' socialization is rarely complete. While fieldworkers submit to the subjects' setting and assume a variety of peripheral and membership roles, they also retain formal ties to the academic world. The socialization of researchers thus retains a dual intentionality. They enter into the world of subjects but remain faithful to their primary goal of research. It is within this context that self-reflection becomes necessary. Thus, researchers must observe the activity of others even while engaging in it. They view self-consciously a world that most subjects take for granted (Hunt, 1984).

The fact that the fieldworker is the primary instrument of inquiry and that fieldwork entails an unusually active, personal, and intellectual commitment has important methodological implications. Researchers' mental experience — however that is defined — mediates their understanding of the cultural and psychological world of subjects. How researchers come to know the world around them and manifest their knowledge in symbolic action helps delineate field relationships. Ultimately, the researcher's subjective experience structures the sociological narrative because it provides the medium through which the raw data is gathered.

This point has been made by a number of fieldworkers in recent years. Thus, Paul Rabinow (1977, p. 151) suggests that even for research, "there is no privileged position, no absolute perspective, and no valid way to eliminate consciousness from our activities or those of others." Both sociologist and members are at once subject and object whose meaningful character is accomplished in relation to each other (Hunt, 1984, p. 285).

In view of the recognition that fieldwork is an interpretive enterprise mediated by the subjective experience of both researcher and subjects, fieldworkers have become increasingly aware of the importance of understanding how their personal experience structures field relations and the kinds of material gathered. However, there is considerable variability in how *researcher subjectivity* is defined. Some accounts view it in terms of the participatory roles adopted in the field, the researcher's reflection about them, and their impact on rapport. Social roles and the self that is embodied in them are taken as the primary units of analysis.

Other studies attempt to include, with varying degrees of success, affective responses in their definition of *subjectivity*. Thus, the roles and activities the researcher assumes are attached to certain feeling states. Existentialists, in particular, express concern with the fit among feelings, symbols, and behaviors in given contexts (Adler and Adler, 1987;

Douglas and Johnson, 1977). Of similar concern is the role of the observer in identifying and empathizing with the observed (Manning, 1987, p. 12). However, there are varying points of view regarding the proper place of any emotion in fieldwork and data gathering. Related to this is a confusion in the literature regarding what kind of researcher behavior constitutes sympathy versus empathy and pathological versus normal involvement. Thus, researchers are often advised to avoid studying cultures about which they have deep emotional conflicts, as if deep conflicts are not mobilized in most research settings (Douglas, 1976; Adler and Adler, 1987; Douglas and Johnson, 1977; Robbins, Anthony, and Curtis, 1973).

Even those sociological accounts which do attempt to consider the affective complexity of researcher subjectivity leave out the role of unconscious processes. Thus, affect, role, and symbolic action are viewed largely as products of taken-for-granted intentionality. These are mediated by interactional and cultural meanings derived from the present rather than the past. One problem in this perspective is that conscious action is reified, and researchers appear as mere caricatures of human beings. At times, they are depicted as rational actors who consciously plan every move they make to further the research goals (Adler and Adler, 1987). At others, they are presented as cunning strategists, sociopaths of sorts, without conscience or inner conflict (Douglas, 1976, 1985).

This is not to suggest that some of these accounts do not imbue the fieldwork with "brute" emotion. Existentialist sociologists, in particular, recognize that irrational feelings seethe beneath the appearance of rational scientific action. The world the researcher encounters is chaotic, irrational, and unpredictable. As a result, the researcher's actions are often spontaneous and emotionally tinged (Adler and Adler, 1987; Douglas and Johnson, 1977). While recognizing that fieldwork involves an irrational dimension, few sociological studies have examined how it structures relations with subjects and the kind of data gathered. Instead, their formal accounts of fieldwork emphasize the intentional strategies used to develop rapport and gather data. As a result, the image of the fieldworker as an oversocialized, manipulative human being is reproduced.

There are a few exceptions, most notably in the recent work of Maurice Punch (1986) and John Van Maanen (1988). Nevertheless, these authors follow their existentialist and symbolic interactionist colleagues by omitting consideration of the unconscious dimension of human interaction. As a result, a coherent theory of fieldwork which considers the impact of irrational forces on field relations and data gathering is left undeveloped.

The following section presents a more detailed overview of how different fieldwork traditions formulate the researcher-subject relationship. The major theoretical and methodological perspectives considered include the classical and symbolic interactionist and the philosophically inspired approaches, in particular the existentialist. Hermeneutic, ethnomethodological, and experiential points of view will be subsumed within the existentialist category, although there are distinctions between them. For present purposes, hermeneutics can be defined as a method of interpretation which stresses holism, context, symbol, and the emergent nature of the ethnographic endeavor. The process of understanding is characterized as a system of circular relations between the whole and its parts. Researchers' meaning worlds and those of subjects accommodate each other dialectically and cannot be understood in separation (Agar, 1980b; Rabinow, 1977). In contrast, ethnomethodologists do not address themselves to the intersubjective nature of ethnography. Instead, they are concerned with developing a full understanding of how subjects construct their social world, unfettered by researchers' preconceptions. The best way to overcome the distortions introduced by outside frames of reference in order to derive a sense of subjects' "first order constructs" is to become the phenomenon of study. Thus, ethnomethodologists encourage fieldworkers to assume membership roles in the researched culture (Mehan and Wood, 1975; Hayano, 1982; Sudnow, 1978). The experiential approach is similar to hermeneutic and ethnomethodological perspectives in that it challenges positivist postulates which stress a separation of subject and object. However, it places particular emphasis on the researcher's personal experience in the field, viewing it as an important source of data about the subjects' psychosocial worlds. Experiential methodologists therefore encourage researchers to be self-reflective and consider themselves as objects of study (Reinharz, 1984).

It should be noted that there are inherent problems in any categorization of fieldwork approaches. The schools discussed represent ideal types which are constituted from selected aspects of the authors' works. Different scholars demonstrate views which do not fit neatly in one category and sometimes overlap several. Despite differences in their epistemological assumptions and views about the role of researcher subjectivity, classical, symbolic interactionist and philosophically inspired methodologies do share a similar disciplinary tradition. In contrast, the psychoanalytic point of view represents a unique approach. This is the result of its special origin in the works of Freud and its recognition that the research and other interpersonal encounters are mediated by unconscious psychological as well as conscious sociological processes.

2. THE SOCIOLOGICAL PERSPECTIVE ON FIELDWORK

Classical and Symbolic Interactionist Perspectives

EPISTEMOLOGICAL ASSUMPTIONS

Early fieldwork studies of the Chicago School were influenced by nineteenth century positivist science and adopted many of its tenets (Park, 1915; Freilich, 1970; Hughes, 1971; Junker, 1960). Classical fieldworkers shared the assumption that there was one reality which existed independently of the researcher's conscious mental activity. In order to develop an accurate understanding of the object of study, researchers were encouraged to maintain a separation between themselves and research subjects. *Researcher subjectivity,* defined as excessive emotional and participatory involvement in the members' world, was viewed as a hindrance to the scientific enterprise. Although Chicago School fieldworkers encouraged students to immerse themselves in the members' natural setting, they worried lest the researchers' affective involvement introduce bias which would undermine scientific objectivity. It was also feared that fieldworkers would be seduced by the subjects' way of life and lose sight of their scientific goals. In the latter case, the researcher and his or her sociological insights would be lost to the scientific community. The best way to minimize the danger of going native or of "overrapport" was for the researcher to assume marginal roles in the setting (Miller, 1952).

The view that fieldworkers should maintain a dichotomy between subject and object by minimizing their involvement in the researched culture and maintaining peripheral roles is implicit in much of the symbolic interactionist literature in sociology (Wax, 1983, p. 192; Shaffir, Stebbins, and Turowetz, 1980, p. 19). A theoretically sophisticated version of this point of view has been articulated by Pollner and

Emerson. They stress that the researcher should maintain a delicate balance between detachment and involvement in fieldwork because, "The epistemology of the social sciences demands the distinction between researchers and researched, observer and observed, and, at the most abstract level, between subject and object. Indeed, the very notion of a science is possible only to the extent that these distinctions can be sustained" (1983, p. 251).

THE ROLE OF AFFECTS AND COGNITION IN FIELDWORK

As the above discussion indicates, researcher subjectivity is viewed by classical and symbolic interactionist scholars as a potential impediment to the fieldwork endeavor because it undermines the researcher's ability to perceive the world in an unbiased fashion. It should be noted, however, that the acceptance of positivist assumptions by classical and some symbolic interactionist researchers does not necessarily reflect their actual fieldwork experience. There is ample evidence in the literature that researchers are not as detached as their formal fieldwork accounts suggest. Thus, classical researchers occasionally over-identify with subjects, lose empathetic communication, react with disgust, anger, infatuation, and fear. However, the irrational feelings that are routinely experienced are rarely subject to serious sociological analysis. While anthropologists appear more willing than sociologists to examine the passions of their scientific pursuits, their discussions generally appear in the form of private diaries, fiction novels, and anecdotal accounts (Malinowski, 1967; Bohannon, 1954; Maybury-Lewis, 1965). Formal narratives about fieldwork are thus separated from the informal discussions of the subjective dimensions of the research encounter, and the myth of researcher objectivity is reproduced (Van Maanen, 1988).

The separation of the fieldworker as emotional and intellectual subject resulted in the development of a peculiar image of researchers as laboratory scientists who, though empathetic, pursue their intellectual goals with little personal passion. They are rational individuals who use their cognitive and intellectual skills to gather data and reflect upon the subjects' world, a domain of experience separate from their own. Classical fieldworkers are also social actors, but their primary point of reference is the world of academia rather than the subjects' culture. They assume marginal roles in the setting but maintain their identity as social scientists and do not attempt to negotiate membership status or conform too dramatically to native norms. In this respect, the secondary socialization of the classical researcher is minimal. Where it occurs, it is instrumental, consciously managed, and does not derive spontaneously from the fieldwork encounter. The classical researcher is therefore a rather simple soul who has a social but no deep inner self. Neither intrapsychic conflicts nor unconscious fantasies mediate the fieldwork encounter.

Some recent studies by symbolic interactionists have attempted to revise the classical image of the "overrational researcher." They depict the researcher as an affective person who inevitably experiences emotional reactions in fieldwork, in view of the deep feelings of insecurity, anxiety, loneliness, frustration, and confusion it engenders (Wax, 1971, p. 20; Schwartz and Schwartz, 1955; Johnson, 1975). However, symbolic interactionists still view these emotional reactions as a hindrance to fieldwork which produces bias and distortion (Wax, 1971, pp. 18-62; Gans, 1968; Denzin, 1970). Lofland, for example, suggests that researchers take account of their private feelings and record them in notes but stresses their disruptive effects on field relations and urges researchers to protect themselves against compromising emotional involvements (Lofland, 1971, p. 131).

Symbolic interactionists also share with classical sociologists a mechanistic view of the researcher. However, this is the result of their dramaturgical metaphor for fieldwork rather than an investment in the laboratory image of the fieldwork setting. The social world is depicted as a stage, and the researcher is an actor. The negotiation of roles in fieldwork is viewed as a conscious process of learning the social script in order to gain access to the backstage regions of the subjects' world. This emphasis on consciousness and intentionality represents both the strength and weakness of the symbolic interactionist approach. On the one hand, researcher behavior is represented as a meaningful product of mental activity. On the other, the researcher is depicted as excessively instrumental and manipulative. The irrational, spontaneous feelings and behaviors which constitute an important aspect of researcher subjectivity are excluded from consideration. The dramatic actor also has no unconscious mental life. Although his or her world is meaningful, its significance is derived from the surface, interactional level of experience. The dramatic actor of the symbolic interactionist therefore resembles the classical laboratory robot. Both are simple persons who have no complex and conflictual inner selves.

Existentialist Perspective

With the advent of phenomenologically inspired studies by sociologists claiming existentialist, ethnomethodological, experiential and hermeneutic perspectives, the epistemological tenets of classical and symbolic interactionist research have been challenged (e.g. Douglas, 1976; Rabinow, 1977; Reinharz, 1984). Phenomenologically inspired studies do not dispute the necessity of constructing a separation of subject and object at different points during the research and writing of materials. However, they argue that the assumption that a dichotomy exists in reality is misleading. At the practical level, it implies that the researcher's adoption of outsider roles in the research setting provides the most objective, scientific data. Although it is likely that the negotiation of insider roles and consequent muting of the subject-object dichotomy threatens empirical objectivity, it is a threat with a corresponding gain. Without formal acknowledgement of the significance of intersubjectivity to the research process itself, empirical objectivity is only attainable at the expense of the object. Recognizing this, existentialists and ethnomethodologists have presented arguments that the assumption of membership roles may facilitate the collection of important materials that would otherwise be inaccessible (Adler and Adler, 1987; Hayano, 1982).

The muting of the subject-object dichotomy is also important in terms of the theoretical analysis of data. Too often the negotiated reality of the ethnographic encounter is attributed to one's informant. In fact, the mental activity of both the researcher and subject mediate the relations between them and define the nature of sociological facts. This is not simply an effect of the roles the researcher assumes, although they clearly have an impact. It also involves subtle dimensions of the research encounter. Thus, the subject-object interaction is mediated by the consciousness and culture of each participation. Regardless of the researchers' actual status, subjects transfer onto them definitions and images that belong to their culture. As a result, subjects are often blind to who the researchers are and what they are actually doing, favoring their own fantasies and notions about them. This process is analogous to the phenomenon of transference in clinical psychoanalysis. The difference is that the meanings attributed to the researcher stem from the subjects' cultural rather than intrapsychic categories, although these are not entirely separate. Obviously, the transference onto the researcher of cultural meanings is linked to the activities, behaviors, and roles the researcher demonstrates. These, in turn, structure the researcher's exposure to different dimensions of the subjects' world (Hunt, 1984).

As researcher and subject get better acquainted, their dialogue changes to reflect different cultural transferences of each participant, and new intersubjective realities emerge. When the researcher leaves the field, these dialogues are reviewed and reinterpreted. Although the subjects are not present to help renegotiate the script, a complex image of them continues to mediate the researcher's interpretation of the data. Thus, even the final construction of the sociological text involves a conversation with a subject.

By automatically assuming a dualism between researcher and subject, the exploration of this complex process of the intersubjective construction of the sociological narrative is made difficult. In contrast, by muting the dichotomy between researcher and subject, fieldwork data can be analyzed in terms of its origin in certain key roles and relationships which develop in the field. Through deconstructing the narrative, researchers will develop a better understanding of the intersubjective process of fieldwork and data construction. From the perspective of existential sociologists, the subject-object dualism is therefore a heuristic device which sometimes aids the analysis of cultural data rather than an objective fact that exists in the external world.

THE ROLE OF AFFECTS AND EMOTIONS

The existentialist awareness that the assumption of a dichotomy between researcher and subjects is problematic in view of the interpretive nature of understanding has led to new insights into the fieldwork endeavor. Existentialist fieldworkers recognize that the research process is far less orderly than is depicted in traditional sociological accounts. Events are often unexpected, irrational, and spontaneous. Researchers are themselves more complex persons than the laboratory robot of the classical tradition or the dramaturgical actor of the symbolic interactionist. Both fieldworker and subjects act on the basis of situated feelings and moods. Sometimes these feelings may dominate the cognitive and intellectual dimensions of consciousness and are prime movers of action (e.g. Douglas, 1976; Cesara, 1982; Johnson,

1975; Douglas and Johnson, 1977; Adler and Adler, 1987; Punch, 1986, Van Maanen, 1988).

The existentialist approach not only recognizes the inevitability of affective involvement in the subject's world but even perceives it as useful to the research enterprise. This latter point in particular distinguishes the existential view from both the classical and symbolic interactionist. By demonstrating certain emotionally mediated behaviors, researchers show they are persons capable of human feelings rather than automatons enacting a prefabricated script. The particular combination of behavior and affect that convinces subjects that the researcher is human varies cross-culturally. However, it is crucial to rapport. Thus, while many traditional sociologists examine researcher behavior in relation to the negotiation of personality traits associated with fieldwork roles, existentialist accounts add that these also involve key emotional dimensions.

Paul Rabinow, an anthropologist of hermeneutic persuasion, provides an interesting example. He relates a series of encounters with Ali, a Moroccan friend and key informant, in which Rabinow became frustrated and angry. They had both been at a wedding. Rabinow became ill and requested to go home. Ali tried to placate him but continued to enjoy the wedding. Finally, at around 3:30 A.M., Rabinow announced he was leaving, thereby forcing Ali to accompany him. During the trip home, Ali kept inquiring if Rabinow was happy. When the enraged anthropologist refused to confirm he was happy, Ali threatened to get out of the car and walk. At one point, Ali opened the door while Rabinow was driving at forty miles an hour. Eventually, Rabinow let Ali out of the car, and Ali walked the remaining five miles home. That evening, Rabinow rehearsed lessons he had learned at the University of Chicago regarding appropriate researcher behavior and found himself wanting. Indeed, he was concerned that his anger had damaged his relationship with Ali and undermined his fieldwork. As it turned out, the opposite resulted. Rabinow's initial passive, scientific stance had been interpreted by his Moroccan informant as a sign of weakness. His subsequent angry and assertive behavior redefined his identity as a man of good character who would not submit to another man's efforts to dominate (Rabinow, 1977, p. 47-48).

After this encounter, Rabinow and Ali's friendship was transformed for the better. They developed a more sharing relationship, and the researcher was exposed to previously hidden dimensions of male culture. For example, he was informed of Ali's involvement with prostitutes and taken to a brothel. It is possible that the same rapport could have been accomplished with less display of frustration. However, it is equally likely that the researcher's investment of his whole person in his actions contributed to the positive transformation of the relationship. Thus, Rabinow's anger was linked to the subtle negotiation of Moroccan male character.

Existentialist sociologists have suggested that the expression of affect in fieldwork may do more than facilitate the negotiation of fieldwork roles and affirm their moral character. It may also provide an important source of cultural data (Reinharz, 1984, p. 336; Hayano, 1982). Riesman (1977), for example, used introspective techniques to examine Fulani social life. He compared his feelings and reactions to particular situations with what he thought the Fulani felt in them. Through this method, he was able to discover some of the rich affectively tinged nuances of the peoples' subjective experiences. He could also understand areas in which his own culturally mediated reactions limited his ability to respond empathetically to members of a uniquely different culture. This book, in particular, illustrates the potential richness of the existentialist approach. In contrast to classical and symbolic interactionist studies, Riesman's ethnography integrates his own reactions and those of Fulani people. He thereby provides a means to simultaneously sort out subject and object while exploring the intersubjective construction of social science data.

THE EXISTENTIAL MODEL OF THE RESEARCHER

The existentialist model of the fieldworker varies with each researcher's account. However, the view which dominates much of the sociological literature is peculiarly incompatible with the authors' stated understanding of the role of the irrational in the fieldwork process. Like the dramatic actor of the symbolic interactionist school, the existentialist sociologist is often presented as self-conscious, over-intentional, and strategic. In accounts of researchers who take the "conflict approach," there is even an ominous thrust to his or her character. He or she is the grand manipulator who comes into the field with multiple strategies to gain the subjects' trust and facilitate entree. For example, in his classic primer on methodology, Jack Douglas (1976) proposes researchers use a variety of techniques to penetrate beyond the frontstage regions of the subjects' world. They are encouraged to infiltrate settings by assuming covert as well as overt identities. They are urged to build "friendly trust" to "open people up." Other recommendations include "setting up" and "discombobulating" subjects. This vision of fieldwork is analogous to guerrilla warfare. Researchers are engaged in planning surprise attacks to catch the subjects off guard. Only then will they gain access to the backstage regions of culture.

It is this element of overintentionality, excessive rationality, and strategic manipulation which differentiates the philosophically inspired views of existential fieldworkers from others who share their epistemological assumptions. For example, studies which take an experiential and hermeneutic approach challenge the subject-object dualism of classical sociology. They are also concerned with researcher subjectivity and recognize the importance of exploring the affective dimensions of the researcher-subject relationship (e.g. Rabinow, 1977; Hunt, 1984; Reinharz, 1984). Hermeneutic studies place particular emphasis on the dynamic nature of the fieldwork process, depicting it as a series of encounters in which both subject and object change and new intersubjective realities emerge (e.g. Hunt, 1984; Rabinow, 1977). At the same time, however, hermeneutic and experiential studies avoid presenting a model of the researcher as either the intellectual robot, overrational actor, or strategic manipulator of the classical, symbolic interactionist and existential traditions in sociological research.

Regardless of these points of difference between the philosophically inspired schools of fieldwork, they are similar in one respect. They share a focus on the social dimensions of the research encounter. Field relationships and data collection are analyzed primarily in terms of the cultural roles and identities which emerge in the fieldwork setting. Rabinow (1977, pp. 5-6), for example, explains that the

> ... self being discussed is perfectly public, it is neither the purely cogito of the Cartesians, nor the deep psychological self of the Freudians. Rather it is the culturally mediated and historically situated self which finds itself in a continuously changing world of meaning.

3. THE PSYCHOANALYTIC PERSPECTIVE ON FIELDWORK

Traditional and contemporary works in the fields of symbolic anthropology display an interest in the application of psychoanalytic ideas to cultural phenomena. In recent years, a few anthropologists have also begun to examine the methodological implications of the psychoanalytic point of view for the relations between researcher and subjects in fieldwork. The psychoanalytic perspective makes three assumptions foreign to most sociologists. First, it assumes that much thought and activity takes place outside of conscious awareness. It follows from this that everyday life is mediated by unconscious images, fantasies, and thoughts. These make their most overt appearance in the jokes, parapraxes, dramatic themes, dreams, fantasies, and affective intonations that punctuate social experience. They can also be disguised more subtly beneath what appears as rational instrumental action. Second, the unconscious meanings which mediate everyday life are linked to complex webs of significance which can ultimately be traced to childhood experiences. Without the benefit of long-term psychoanalytic treatment, these connections can only be inferred from surface derivatives. Nevertheless, the psychoanalytic perspective assumes that *transferences,* defined as the imposition of archaic (childhood) images onto present day objects, are a routine feature of most relationships. While they add richness and depth to many, they hinder the development of closeness and trust in others. In either case, transferences structure social relationships in particular ways.

Third, psychoanalysis is a theory of intrapsychic conflict. It postulates that the human psyche is functionally divided into a tripartite system composed of the id, ego, and superego. The individual's libidinal or aggressive desires are often in conflict with the demands of the ego, that part of the mental apparatus which mediates between the id and the outside world. Related to this is the conflict that may emerge between individual and society. The demands of reality sometimes conflict with desire. Adjustments are made which serve the interests of survival but do not necessarily enhance individual pleasure or creativity. Conflict may also occur between the superego, defined as the ideal self, and internalized parental norms, the ego, and id. Intrapsychic conflict is routinely mobilized in relation to external events, in particular those that arouse anxiety or link to unresolved issues from childhood. The concept of compromise formation is relevant here. Inner conflicts that are routinely experienced by individuals in the course of their everyday lives are resolved in the form of compromises between wishes, defenses, and internalized moral demands. Most products of mental activity — including art and symbolic communication — may, upon deeper investigation, reveal hidden aggression, forbidden desire, and defenses against these wishes.

Psychoanalytic approaches to fieldwork methodology take these three assumptions into account in their examination of researcher-subject relations. Thus, while existentialist and hermeneutic accounts focus on the cultural dimensions of the fieldwork encounter, psychoanalytic studies examine the intrapsychic. The encounter between researcher and subjects is read as a script which contains a latent psychological as well as a manifest cultural content. Transferences are assumed to mediate the relationship between researcher and subjects. Symbolic interaction, traditionally viewed by sociologists in terms of its cultural and behavioral dimensions, can be interpreted as a complex exchange of unconscious fantasies. Similarly, it is possible to analyze symbolic acts of both researcher and subjects as compromise formations which embody hidden desires and defenses.

As the above discussion indicates, psychoanalysis is a theory of normal as well as pathological thought and behavior. It assumes that for all individuals, unconscious fantasy is a feature of mental life which accompanies conscious experience. This point is particularly important to stress, since readers unfamiliar with the perspective might be tempted to interpret a description of the unconscious dynamics of the research encounter as peculiar, bizarre, or pathological, thereby omitting consideration of the way that transferences routinely mediate everyday life among all persons in natural and research settings.

The psychoanalytic examination of fieldwork is important because it contributes to our understanding of the structuring of social science data. For example, the unconscious communications which are negotiated in the research encounter effect empathy and rapport. They therefore play a role in the materials that subjects reveal and researchers grasp. The transference reactions that are mobilized in fieldwork may facilitate researchers' understanding of certain dimensions of the subjects' world while blinding them to others. Intrapsychic issues also affect the methodologies that researchers employ and the kind of data gathered. For example, scientific methodologies which rely on structured interviews may conceal transferences and serve defensive purposes. While researchers appear to be gathering objective data, they are also avoiding closeness to subjects that may create anxiety. This results in the gathering of data that is often far removed from the meaningful world of subjects (Devereux, 1967).

As the above discussion indicates, the psychoanalytic perspective results in a unique interpretation of researcher subjectivity in fieldwork. Existential and hermeneutic accounts generally define researcher subjectivity in relation to the fieldworkers' conscious experiences, feeling states, and participatory cultural roles. Reflection about the researcher's activities and reactions is assumed to provide data regarding the social and emotional world of subjects. This is particularly likely when the researcher shares the subjects' world and is socialized into their culture. The psychoanalytic anthropologist, in contrast, views researcher subjectivity in terms of unconscious processes that mediate the relationship between researcher and subject. Intrapsychic processes within the researcher effect empathy and structure field relationships. As a result, introspection is as important a tool in research as self-reflection. The researcher's associations to experiences that evoke anxiety, boredom, anger, or love, for example, may provide clues regarding transference reactions which hinder empathetic understanding. The analysis of dreams, parapraxes, and fantasies may provide a useful means to facilitate the exploration of the unconscious dynamics of the subject-object relationship.

Existentialist fieldworkers do acknowledge the role of irrational thoughts and feelings in fieldwork. However, they are vague about their constitution. On the one hand, we are told that the irrational is inevitable in research. On the other, we are instructed that fieldworkers should avoid studying people about whom they experience deep conflicts (Adler and Adler, 1987; Douglas, 1976). Psychoanalytic anthropologists, in contrast, specifically link irrational forces to unconscious fantasy life. They assume that inner conflicts are inevitably mobilized in any research setting. First, complex motivations structure the researcher's choice of setting. Second, situational and relational encounters in fieldwork may evoke intrapsychic conflict at different points in the research. The researcher's task is to examine how such transferences structure relations with subjects rather than assume there are field settings and situations in which they can be avoided.

This does not deny that some researchers are psychologically better suited to study some settings than others. It simply suggests that, at one time or another, deeply rooted conflicts will be mobilized in any setting. In long-term, intensive fieldwork, it is probably impossible to avoid periodically slipping into what Jack Douglas (1985) refers to as the "black hole" of the past. In some cases, in fact, certain behaviors engaged in during fieldwork may involve a repetition in action of repressed memories and unconscious fantasies. These actions may be useful to the fieldwork endeavor because they facilitate the negotiation of trustworthy membership roles. For example, police researchers who take action to back up their partner or help a victim may be enacting an unconscious rescue fantasy that links to childhood images (Freud, 1910; Esman, 1987). At the same time, they are engaging in behaviors which police admire and which enhance their status among them (Van Maanen, 1978; Hunt, 1984). The researcher's unconscious fantasies may also facilitate rapport if they resonate with similar fantasies of subjects. At other times, the enactment of unconscious fantasies in fieldwork may interfere with research relations. This is the case if the resultant behaviors are culturally dystonic or reduce the researcher's ability to be empathetic and personally flexible.

EPISTEMOLOGICAL ASSUMPTIONS

With few exceptions, most notably in the work of LeVine (1982) and Devereux (1967), psychoanalytic anthropologists assume the epistemological perspective of existential and hermeneutic researchers (Crapanzano, 1980; Kracke, 1987a). They recognize that the assumption of a dualism between researcher and subject is problematic in view of the interpretive nature of the research endeavor. Psychoanalytic anthropologists also stress the dynamic quality of field relations and data gathering. The fieldworker's journey involves a complex transformation in the subject, object, and known cultural reality. The cultural narrative is complex and multilayered. From moment to moment, week to week, and year to year, it fluctuates. Cultural and psychological motifs which appear dominant at one point in time recede into the background at another. As a result, the scientific accounts of both social and intrapsychic worlds are inevitably partial and incomplete. The accounts suspend each narrative world for observation, bracketing the ebb and flow of daily life and thought as if they were static and unchanging. The "mythical" quality of scientific accounts is more dramatic when we consider the fact that they are mediated by the researcher's own interpretations of what constitutes the dominant themes at the time the researcher collects the data, reviews the materials, and writes the account. Finally, the scientific accounts which emerge from the fieldwork setting reflect the reality of neither the subject nor the object. They emerge out of a complex dialogue which changes through time as each person is transformed in the encounter with the other.

The clinical encounter in psychoanalysis can be viewed in a similar manner as the cultural. However, the unconscious dimensions of the dialogue constitute the essential transformative dynamic. Thus, the analyst listens to the patient's narrative, makes connections, and provides interpretations. Periodically, countertransferences, defined as the analyst's unconscious, conflictual response to the patient's transference, arise and hinder understanding. The analyst explores these reactions and, in so doing, transforms his or her own intrapsychic self. This change then facilitates a renewed empathetic communication with the analysand and, ultimately, aids in the formulation of interpretations. The resultant insight leads to a change in the patient's inner world, his or her transference to the analyst, and the narrative which contains derivatives of both. At some point, countertransferences are once again mobilized and analyzed and empathetic communication regained. This process is repeated over again and forms the fundamental dynamic of the psychoanalytic encounter. The psychoanalytic process is therefore hermeneutic. Analysts discover and transform themselves in the therapeutic interaction with the other. The psychoanalytic narrative thus constitutes an intersubjective construction mediated by the shifting conscious and unconscious mental representations, transferences, and countertransferences of both analyst and analysand.

While hermeneutic and existential sociologists accept a dynamic model of the fieldwork process, they omit consideration of the intrapsychic dimension. Psychoanalytic anthropologists accept the hermeneutic paradigm but recognize that the ethnographic encounter involves unconscious as well as cultural dimensions. Thus, unconscious as well as cultural meanings mediate the researcher's interpretation of the subjects' world. Changes in the researcher's and subjects' "selves" occur at both intrapsychic and cultural levels.

Fieldwork and the Mobilization of Intrapsychic Conflict

FIELDWORKERS' CHOICE OF SETTING

The unconscious structuring of fieldwork begins prior to the initiation of research. The choice of setting itself may reflect an inner dynamic. While any researcher's interest in a particular topic is structured by rational and instrumental factors, additional motives are often at work. My own curiosity about police culture, for example, did not begin with a literature review. It grew out of a dramatic exposure to the subjects. I was a graduate student in anthropology attempting to teach my first college class. My students were police officers and my classroom the 103rd Precinct in Queens, New York. It was during the early

1970s. Thomas Shea, an officer in the precinct, was under investigation for shooting a ten-year-old boy named Clifford Glover. Racial tensions were high in the Queens community. The police felt the precinct was under siege. An aura of social conflict and violence clearly mediated my first exposure to the cultural world of the police.

Needless to say, I found myself somewhat intimidated when I walked in the classroom and faced forty armed men, most dressed in Levis and flannel shirts. I had long been active in the antiwar movement and was usually on the opposite side of the picket line from the men I faced that day. I hid behind the podium for the duration of the semester, a fact that eventually became the object of some police humor. By midsemester, the police had grown fond of me and I of them. Eventually, several concerned officers inquired sheepishly if I had been at the "wrong end" of their sticks during the 1968 "riot" at Columbia University.

However, my associations to police extended further back in the past than even the antiwar movement. The armed men I faced brought to mind many exciting images which indirectly involved members of my family. The subject of cops and robbers, for example, brought forth a memory of my older brother and me, pretending to be Bonnie and Clyde as we walked away from the movie theatre. One police student, who wore strings of bullets across his chest, reminded me of the Mexican revolutionary Emilio Zapata, whose picture had decorated the walls of my college room. Another bearded officer bore a remarkable resemblance to Che Guevera, an important hero of my youth. Like my father, Che was a medical doctor and a political leftist. My father is a psychiatrist. Like Freud, Che wore a beard.

These memories of the facts and fantasies which accompanied my first encounter with police represent only the surface of the complex threads which linked me to them. Nevertheless, even these surface associations suggest that my romance with the police began long before I laid eyes on my fieldwork subjects. The unconscious fantasies which were mobilized in my first encounter served to fuel my curiosity and even direct the focus of my research. Thus, I developed a particular interest in exploring what lay beneath these presumed violent and powerful men who played such a contradictory role in society, and possibly in my unconscious. Along these lines, it is probably not accidental that my best-known work on police concerns their use of force (Hunt, 1985).

There are few researchers whose object of study does not condense a richly colored prism of transferences. Hayano (1982), for example, traces his interest in the world of gambling to his childhood. Although his parents neither smoked, drank, nor gambled, he, nevertheless, developed an active interest in magic and card tricks and enjoyed playing card games with his siblings. Hayano's desire to explore the world of gambling was partly rooted in a childhood identification with the television character Maverick. He explains, "I often fancied myself roaming from town to town playing poker and winning hundreds of dollars. Inside my expensive silk shirt, like Maverick's, was pinned a thousand dollar bill for emergencies."

Anthropologist Obeyesekere (1981) locates his interest in ecstatic priests to an encounter with Karunaviti women which produced disgust and anxiety. He associated the matted locks of the female ecstatics to Medusa's head and Freud's essay on the subject, which largely concerns male fears of castration (Freud, 1922). In the absence of more detailed associations, it is not possible to determine the genetic sources of Obeyesekere's curiosity. Snake-haired women condense a Rorschach of multiple meanings which both fascinate and repel. Medusa's head, for example, could evoke other images besides castration. To some, the whiplike shape and movement of her hair might suggest a sadomasochistic encounter. The snakes' poisonous, biting fangs could evoke oral images of being attacked and devoured. The phallic aspect of these dancing women could link to preoedipal and oedipal fantasies of paternal as well as maternal seduction. In any case, Obeyesekere does indicate that his initial emotional and associative relation to the Hindu women led to the formulation of his "Medusa hypothesis" and a whole line of fruitful research (Obeyesekere, 1981, pp. 6-7).

One sociologist began her fieldwork with a strong interest in the political economy of class, race, and gender and intended to do a study of women's roles. However, she collected extensive data on the subject of poverty and housing and eventually decided to study that subject. Certain fieldwork dreams which preceded the change in research focus possibly shed light on its unconscious dynamics. One dream took place after the researcher returned to India from a brief vacation in the United States. At that time, she found herself forced to live with her husband in a small, crowded dwelling. This experience appeared to mobilize transferences alluded to in the dream. Thus, she associated the dream to a difficult period in her childhood in which she and her family lived in a small apartment and her parents fought a great deal. Her object of study may have evolved, in part, out of a complex effort to understand

and master these painful aspects of her past. In an interview with this author, the sociologist discusses the dream and several associations.

> I woke up very tired, especially my eyes. I dreamed that people were being beaten on the subway and of 45 Crimson Avenue which was being turned into a condominium. Nothing comes to mind about the dream. 45 Crimson Avenue is not a place that I would want to go back to. It's where I grew up. My parents now live in a co-op which is a little like a condo I guess. My parents did quarrel a lot when I was a child. There was a lot of fighting. We also lived in this very small place. It was just a few rooms and it was very crowded. . . . It's funny because John (her husband) and I had just moved into a two room dwelling in India to do the research. Maybe that made me anxious.

Finally, Waud Kracke, a psychoanalytically trained anthropologist, provides convincing evidence that his choice of research setting and subject of inquiry was structured by complex unconscious issues, revolving around oedipal themes in particular.[1] Kracke conducted long-term fieldwork among South American Indians. The Indians were former headhunters, and Kracke was interested in exploring patterns of leadership. Castration concerns and competition with father imagos constitute important themes in his research (Kracke, 1987a).

Kagwahiv people appear unusual because they express openly in daily life mythology and dreams, feelings, and fantasies that are generally disguised in Euro-American culture. Memories of sexual curiosity and even childhood oedipal fantasies, for example, are openly available to consciousness. Kracke's interviews about these fantasies in particular provided a vehicle for getting in touch with certain aspects of his inner self and alerted him to the unconscious structuring of his choice of research subject. Kracke explains:

> But I have only gradually discovered the extent to which their expression of these themes became a vehicle for vicarious expression of my own fantasy life. Even now, in intense periods of working through conflicts, I find myself practically redreaming the dreams that were told to me by Jovenil or Francisco — if not literally in the manifest content of my own dreams, at least taking a very important place in the latent content. I am sure at some level I was seeking something like this when I chose to work with South American Indians in the first place, no doubt especially when I selected a group of former headhunters for my study. But the point here is the degree to which the experience was integrated into my personal-

ity—through my transference to Jovenil and, to a lesser extent, to Francisco and Mōhagi and others (1987a, p. 77).

While, the unconscious fantasies that are mobilized in the initial research encounter sometimes interfere with scientific understanding, they often add richness, depth, and meaning. They may also provide an essential motivating force to facilitate the accomplishment of research, among difficult groups in particular. Thus, the Yanomamo Indians (Chagnon, 1974, 1968), Hell's Angels (Thompson, 1967), and Nazi doctors (Lifton, 1986), would not likely be the subject of much serious investigation without a push from mental forces which violate the canons of rational, instrumental action. It should be noted that unconscious fantasy plays a role in quantitative as well as qualitative research in natural and social science disciplines. For example, Jules Glenn (1984) discusses the analytic treatment of a scientist whose theory of the origin of a particular disease was partly rooted in a complex unconscious fantasy.

INSIDE THE RESEARCH SETTING

Once the researcher has immersed himself or herself in the particular setting and begun relationships with subjects, unconscious factors continue to mediate the fieldwork encounter. These may be activated in relation to a variety of situations which link to childhood memories and mobilize transferences. "Culture shock," the experience of being a stranger in an alien and unfamiliar world, is one situation. The roles the researcher assumes in the research setting may also induce regression and evoke transferences. Exposure to anxiety-producing images involving illness, injury, and death often create anxiety, in part because they connect to deeply rooted wishes and fears. Finally the subjects' behavior and unconscious transferences toward the researcher may generate the development of reciprocal reactions and transferences.

The mobilization of transferences in fieldwork is important to understand because it may result in the construction of defensive measures to avoid the problematic situation. For example, a fieldworker might utilize behavioral and methodological techniques to increase distance from subjects when the signal of anxiety is experienced. The researcher's transference reactions might inhibit empathetic communication with subjects. Distortions may be introduced and the researcher blinded to important dimensions of the subjects' world. Transferences may help structure the kinds of roles that fieldworkers assume and the flexibility of their related behaviors. Ultimately, the transferences situationally mobilized in the fieldwork encounter may have an impact on the kinds of relations which develop in fieldwork and structure the data gathered (Devereux, 1967).

CULTURE SHOCK

Immersion in an alien culture is an intense experience. Most researchers report feeling some mixture of confusion, anxiety, excitement, frustration, depression, and embarrassment. This subjective experience has been commonly termed "culture shock" (Kracke, 1987a, p. 60). The experience of culture shock is most dramatic in cross-cultural fieldwork. However, it also characterizes some aspects of the sociologist's encounter with more familiar native subcultures. Numerous researchers have commented on the regressive reactions that accompany, in particular, the initial weeks in the field. Some of the researchers' discomfort stems from the fact that they have lost their bearings, do not know how to communicate in the new setting, and often feel like helpless children (Caudill, 1961; Bohannon, 1954; Briggs, 1970). The researcher's conscious sense of discomfort links to unconscious issues that reveal themselves in dreams and fantasies. Waud Kracke, for example, notes that recurring themes of his dreams during the initial stages of fieldwork were a sense of helplessness or frustration at not being able to understand or do what needed to be done. In one dream, he pulls out money to pay the bill in an unknown Italian city, only to find he has dollars and cruzeiros but no lire. In other dreams, he has to perform tasks he is not prepared for, like flying a plane or performing a part in an unfamiliar play (Kracke, 1987a, pp. 70-71).

Similar kinds of dreams punctuated the initial months of my fieldwork among Metro City Police and continued to emerge in the context of dangerous encounters which generated anxiety. Like Kracke, I had dreams in which I was called upon to engage in activity for which I felt ill-equipped. In one dream, a man fired shots at me and my female partner. It was not clear if I could protect us because the gun she handed me was unloaded or the grips were too small. Following police rules and regulations, I called an assist officer. When I sought support for my actions from the Police Commissioner, he was nowhere to be found.

Whatever their roots in the reality of the day residue, both my and Kracke's dreams demonstrate some typical unconscious fantasies that may be mobilized in the cultural encounter. In Kracke's case, phallic inferiority and oedipal issues appear dominant. Thus, he is unable to assume a number of key, masculine roles, such as being the pilot and paying the bill. The common unconscious equation between phallus, money, and feces is apparent in the latter dream (Freud, 1909; Shengold, 1980). Thus, Kracke's money is symbolically viewed as worthless in the culture of research. My own dreams reflect similar kinds of fantasies but are gender-specific. In particular, the dilemma of being a female researcher in a male-dominated culture appeared to generate a desire for "masculine" power, unconscious guilt about aggression, and a sense of feminine lack. In effect, I had not been given the proper "phallic" equipment to adequately fulfill the role of police researcher and protect myself against danger.

These dreams not only reveal universal themes alive in the unconscious of most men and women but also condense specific referents from the dreamer's past. Only the dreamers' associations would provide the clues necessary to determine the latter. However, Kracke does note one childhood relationship that assumed importance in the initial stages of the cultural encounter. The irritability that surrounded his difficulty communicating in the native language reflected a pattern of interaction tinged with sibling rivalry that he had with his younger sister (Kracke, 1987a, p. 67).

Other anxieties researchers experience in the initial phases of fieldwork may result from the loss experienced when they leave their native culture behind. Some researchers have compared culture shock to dying. Important objects, ideas, and people which provided an integrated sense of body ego and identity are lost (Garza-Guerrera, 1974; Wengle, 1984). From this perspective, socialization into the culture of study may involve a process of mourning. Thus, anthropologists have reported that initial fieldwork dreams and fantasies often involve images of longed-for people, objects, and food (Kracke, 1987, p. 69; Anderson, 1971). Researchers also report frequent anxieties about body health which confirm that concerns about "castration" and loss of bodily integrity are important features of the fieldwork encounter (Kracke, 1987a).

One researcher I interviewed reported a dream that illustrates some universal features of culture shock while placing them in the context of the dreamer's unique childhood experience. In doing so, they reveal the way transference fantasies are situationally generated in the fieldwork encounter. The researcher was taking his first trip to Africa, which he initially experienced as a strange and somewhat dangerous place. After wandering about Nairobi for several hours, he encountered an African man who guided him to the home of a native family who provided food and shelter. That night, the researcher had a dream in which he was taking a shower in Coca-Cola.

> I was taking a shower in Coca-Cola. I remember putting my face up and it was Coca-Cola and I was thrilled. I remember drinking the water, the Coke, and I wasn't thirsty anymore. It was a powerful image.

In recounting the dream, the researcher thought of his childhood in the southern United States where Coke was an important thirst-quenching drink. He recalled an incident when he was thirteen years old in which a biology teacher had taken him to the cola factory to buy "an original Coke." The original Coke turned out to be a blown-up R.C. Cola bottle, a smaller replica of which he still kept in his room. The researcher also remembered an encounter with a ninth-grade, advanced-placement history teacher. The teacher had explained to the class that Coca-Cola was a man's favorite drink because the bottle was shaped like a woman. The researcher recalled that the history teacher did not seem like "a serious scholar." In contrast, he was "attractive" and resembled the male strippers from Chippendale's, about whom his girlfriend had told him.

The dream speaks to the stranger's sense of loss in the face of an alien world and desire for the familiar objects of home and childhood. Certainly, Coca-Cola is a key symbol of American as well as southern culture. The dream also displays castration concerns which were partly resolved through the invention of the large and powerful R.C. "cock" bottle. The cultural encounter and the castration threats it mobilized appeared to result in a partial retreat from heterosexuality. Thus, the dream reveals strong desires to be loved and protected by men in particular. From this perspective, the Coca-Cola which quenches the dreamer's thirst could represent fellatio, the bottle a phallus, and the cola in which he showers, a sticky substance like semen. The history teacher who is recalled in the dreamer's associations represents the most overt object of desire.

Like most dreams, the Coca-Cola dream is a compromise formation which contains contradictory wishes and defenses. The desire for a large penis for self-protection and sexual satisfaction dominates the dream and its associations. However, it also disguises positive oedipal wishes. For example, the teachers who provide the Coke power also instruct the dreamer about women. Thus, the biology professor usually educates children about female anatomy and sexuality. In the dream associations, the history teacher directly tells the dreamer about "real men's" desires when he compares the Coke bottle to a woman's body. The invention of the girlfriend in the dreamer's associations following mention of Chippendale's also represents a fulfillment of heterosexual wishes as well as a defense against awareness of homosexual desire. Even the wish to incorporate the father's penis may be associated with the positive oedipal phase and be consistent with heterosexual object choice. In particular, it can represent an attempt to acquire the father's prowess, become like him, and take his place. Finally, for the dreamer of the Coca-Cola dream, the experience of culture shock may have also mobilized a deeper wish to be nurtured by a maternal person. Thus, in the complex and many layered language of the dream symbol, the Coke bottle could represent a special childhood drink, a penis, a woman, and perhaps the mother's breast as well.

RESEARCHER ROLES

The roles researchers assume in fieldwork may also induce regression and generate the development of transferences. This is particularly likely if the role links to problematic repressed memories and becomes imbedded in conflict. In that case, the culture of research becomes equated with the individual's family, and subjects become the object of unconscious fantasies. Along these lines, anthropologists frequently talk about being "adopted" by members of the culture of study (Briggs, 1970). This metaphor is multidetermined but partly alludes to the complex way that wishes generated in a family context can impose themselves on the ongoing cultural encounter.

Researchers generally negotiate a variety of roles during any period of participant observation. Initially, most begin their tenure as outsiders to the culture of study. Some researchers do not find such marginal roles troublesome. This is the case if they conform with certain methodological assumptions, fit the goals of the research, and are consistent with personal preferences. The maintenance of a marginal status may also serve defensive purposes by protecting the researcher against closeness to subjects, which causes anxiety. Other fieldworkers feel that peripheral membership roles adversely affect the gathering of in-depth field data by limiting access to the backstage regions of the subject's world (Adler, 1987; Punch, 1978; Van Maanen, 1978; Hunt, 1984). Furthermore, the anxiety generated by being an outsider can intensify if it links to unconscious conflicts in the researcher.

There are a number of common childhood experiences and fantasies that could be mobilized in relation to the marginal roles researchers assume in the initial stages of fieldwork. The birth of a younger sibling, for example, may be unconsciously tied to some researchers' experience of being an outsider in fieldwork. Thus, sibling birth is often experienced by older children as a dethronement in which they lose their special place within the family. Children may attribute their loss in family status to any combination of factors. It may be viewed as punishment for unacceptable aggressive or libidinal wishes towards parents or siblings. If the new sibling is of a different gender, the child may fantasize that biological sex is responsible for his or her displacement.

It is possible, for example, that the issue of sibling birth was a hidden theme mobilized in the Coca-Cola dream. When he first arrives in Africa, the researcher describes some of the typical feelings associated with "culture shock," including intense loneliness and alienation. He seems to feel as if he is an orphan in the social world in which he wanders. In an association which provides the narrative frame for the dream, he mentions meeting a native family. They provide a "special" room for him in their home, and he is greatly comforted. However, he also feels guilty about displacing someone else. One person who could be condensed in the image of the displaced person could be a sibling who the dreamer wished to get rid of in order to have his father's love to himself. In this case, the two male teachers in the dreamer's associations could symbolize father figures. The dreamer's wish to be his father's favorite child is fulfilled in the latent content of the dream. He is the one who is provided the R.C. Cola bottle, rather than his sibling-classmates. Dream images are highly condensed, and other meanings are salient.

Childhood fantasies of castration may also be evoked in fieldwork in the context of the researcher's status as a powerless, low-caste stranger. These were evident in Waud Kracke's dreams previously cited. Castration fantasies are gender-specific in content and vary between girls and boys. The fantasy constellation surrounding issues of castration in girls is commonly referred to as "penis envy" or the "castration complex." For present purposes, these concepts can best be understood as metaphors for a complex system of power relations which exist at both cultural and unconscious levels. They have roots in a childhood fantasy of being injured or lacking something which provides status, power, and protection. They may also be based on the girl's actual experience of relationships in the family and larger social world which affirm her sense that femininity is devalued (Freud, 1920; Mitchell, 1974; Grossman and Steward, 1977; Blum, 1977; Hunt and Rudden, 1986).

Fieldwork in some institutional settings is highly stratified by rank and gender. In these settings in particular, a female researcher's experience of marginality and low status may link to any number of fantasies, including those surrounding the castration complex. If the fieldwork experience duplicates in actuality childhood traumas, then the researcher's emotional discomfort is likely to increase. Unfortunately, most researchers have not collected the kinds of data which would facilitate the development of an in-depth understanding of the link between unconscious processes and the fieldwork experience. As a result, this discussion can only be speculative. However, the way that researchers manage the transferences that mediate research roles has an important impact on field relations. Researchers' unconscious desire to have status and/or a sense of belonging in their own family, for example, may act as an impetus for negotiating key membership roles in the culture of study. This is not the only root of the researcher's choice of role. It is also structured by conscious efforts to gain trust, situational exigencies, and secondary socialization into the subject's culture. However, the enormous variety of roles different researchers assume in similar settings indicate that unconscious factors may play a part in the researcher's behavior.

My research among the police presented a number of special problems which made the development of rapport particularly difficult and also exacerbated inner tensions. First, no neutral category of researcher existed within the subjects' frame of reference. Initially, most officers thought I was a spy, armed with a hidden tape recorder, who would expose their participation in corruption and brutality. Consequently, I was greeted in a hostile manner by some and entertained with long periods of silence by others. Gender was also a factor which mediated my fieldwork status and was often problematic. Thus, for a variety of psychological and cultural reasons, the police were threatened by the presence of a feminine woman in their domain. As a result, I was subjected to various sexualized behaviors which served to defend the police against the symbolic threat I represented (Hunt, in press, 1984).

My status as an unwanted, female outsider appeared to mobilize a number of unconscious issues for me as well as for the police. The management of these issues partly structured the roles I negotiated as the fieldwork progressed and informed my access to research subjects. For example, I suspect that the actual experience of being treated as a devalued woman with outsider status linked to deeper issues from my past. These partly revolved around a sense of displacement which accompanied the birth of my brother and may have been linked to gender. My assumption of an androgynous research role, which combined masculine characteristics admired by police with feminine ones, possibly represented an effort to compete in my family as well as the world of the police. By being part boy, I imagined that I could avoid displacement by sibling rivals and gain my father's approval. In this case, the police represented paternal transference figures.

Positive oedipal wishes also appeared to be mobilized in the fieldwork encounter. The resultant anxieties were increased because of the proportion of men to women in the police organization and the way in which policemen sexualized so many encounters. Policemen traditionally protect their wives and families from the realities of their occupational life. The fact that I knew more about their work world than their wives also may have heightened anxiety because it implied closeness to subjects. By partly defeminizing myself through the adoption of a liminal gender role, I avoided a conflictual oedipal victory.

That the police represented forbidden objects of sexual desire was revealed in dreams and slips of the tongue. For example, I recall one conversation with female officers concerning the professional attributes of an attractive male member of their squad. I agreed with the policewomen's assessment of their colleague and tried to say a few words in his favor. Much to the women's amusement and my chagrin, the intended sentence "Jim's a good cop" came out instead "Jim's a good cock." In those words, I revealed my sexual interest in a category of men who were forbidden as a result of their status as research subjects. In that way, they resembled incestuous objects.

As the above discussion suggests, the roles researchers negotiate often serve a variety of unconscious purposes. This does not negate the usefulness of these roles, but simply adds a complex dimension to our understanding of them. I was studying a world largely composed of men who viewed femininity in conflict with key occupational skills. Women were also threatening figures who evoked images of exposure and castration (Hunt, in press). My demonstration of "masculine" personality traits and abilities therefore enhanced the policemen's trust in me as well as my status among them (Hunt, 1984). Through the negotiation of a complex role that combined elements of masculinity and femininity, I was allowed access to the informal dimensions of police culture denied certain traditional categories of women.

At the same time a research role enhances access to some dimensions of the subjects' world, it blinds the researcher to others. This is likely when certain aspects of the role serve defensive purposes to repress forbidden wishes. In this case, the role cannot be easily discarded without psychological risk, and the researcher's flexibility and empathetic capacities may be inhibited. In my research among police, I suspect I was blinded to certain dimensions of the subjects' world which might have been available to me or another researcher who managed intrapsychic conflicts in alternative ways. For example, my data on some categories of women in the policeman's universe is limited. The "ultrafeminine" policewomen who demonstrated stereotypical feminine behavior and little job competence have a relatively negligible place in my fieldnotes. In contrast, women who appeared both feminine and competent are far better represented. This omission resulted from the fact that none of the ultrafeminine women became my key informants. Thus, although I rode and talked to many ultrafeminine policewomen who composed the research sample, I did not develop the kind of close relationships with them experienced with certain other officers.

My data on police is also less abundant than it could have been, in view of the opportunities available. I was invited to the homes of several male officers to meet their wives and families but usually declined the invitations. Rationally, I justified my action on the basis of time limitations and what I perceived as my research goals. In fact, the idea of having dinner with policemen's families outside the district context made me uncomfortable. My anxieties about meeting police wives and lapse of empathy with certain kinds of policewomen related to many issues. Foremost was a possible unconscious fear that the androgynous status which protected me against oedipal concerns and allowed me a special place among the police would be undermined by exposure to the domestic world of women.

It is not uncommon for researchers to have different interpretations of similar settings (Lewis, 1963; Redfield, 1973; Mead, 1923; Freeman, 1983). The reasons for this are complex, and historical and social factors certainly play important roles. There is also little doubt that the sociological narrative is partly autobiographical, reflecting something about the researcher's personality as well as those of the subjects who enter the ethnographic dialogue. From this perspective, fieldwork is, in part, the discovery of the self through the detour of the other (Rabinow, 1977; Crapanzano, 1980; Ricoeur, 1970).

My interpretation of policewomen, for example, was structured by unconscious factors which partly related to the roles I assumed in their setting. Thus, I first saw in policewomen the complex negotiations of masculine and feminine gender symbols and behaviors that were subsequently noted in myself (Hunt, in press, 1984). My writings reflect this insight and, in contrast to other accounts of police, indicate that women play a role in their dramas of violence and lying (Hunt, 1985; Hunt and Manning, in press). Similarly, my interpretation of the social construction of gender in women in transitional occupations contrasts with many previous studies. The latter tend to view male and female worlds as rigidly divided, dichotomous, and unnegotiable (Martin, 1980). In contrast, I saw more androgynous gender behaviors displayed by both sexes. Women, in particular, attempted to negotiate new definitions of femininity which involved valued male and female behaviors (Hunt, in press). A recent work by Lynn Zimmer (1986) on prison guards is innovative because it also notes the way women in a male-dominated world construct new cultural categories of gender (Hunt, 1987). In cases in which researchers discover new dimensions of reality about which others have been blinded, problematic transferences may have been understood. Alternatively, unconscious fantasies which structured their own fieldwork roles may have played a creative role in the perception and analysis of the data.

Once the researcher has achieved some kind of membership status and the anxiety surrounding marginality has diminished, new problems may arise and additional transferences be mobilized which structure research relations. Waud Kracke provides examples from his fieldwork among the Kagwahiv of Brazil. He had spent approximately three months in the field when he was asked to assume an important medical role in the treatment of the daughter and father of Jovenil, a key informant. Around this time, he had the following dream.

First, at home, I was about to begin the dress rehearsal of a play in which I was playing the lead (Romeo), but I had not even read through my part, much less learned my lines. In the other scene I was visiting my analyst, and suddenly realized that in waiting for him I was sitting in his chair, writing things (as I was writing my field notes in my hammock last night), and hastily got out of it as I heard him come in. In association, I had a fantasy that Manzinho's father, "being chief here," folded up a lot of plastic canvas I had on my porch; and some thoughts about the difficulty I had been having the last few days in getting up "to do daily chores such as injections" (Kracke, 1985, pp. 18-19).

Without more knowledge of the dreamer's associations and his past and present life, it is difficult to interpret the dream with much precision. However, several themes stand out which suggest that assuming a key, participatory role mobilized oedipal wishes and fears. The request that Kracke assume the position of doctor thus appeared to link to paternal transferences towards his own analyst, "the real doctor," and Jovenil, the fieldwork father imago. In the first scene, the dreamer expresses the desire to be the lover, Romeo. The next scene depicts his wish to take his analyst's place, sit in his chair, and take notes. Apparently, the fulfillment of these oedipal wishes to become the "doctor" (i.e. father) and "give the injections" (engage in sexual activity) evoked castration fears that had to be defended against. Kracke thus arranges his own defeat in the dream and his associations to it. The dreamer is ill-equipped to play the role of Romeo. He does not know his lines. His power is also symbolically deflated when the "real chief" folds the plastic canvas that rests on the porch. In this context, the porch appears to symbolize the dreamer's body and the expandable canvas a phallic extension of it.

Kracke's introspective awareness and ability to resolve the inner tensions that were aroused in the fieldwork encounter had important ramifications for his methodology and data collection. He was able to comfortably assume the designated role of healer and abandon certain methodological procedures which enhanced distance from feared transference figures. The latter transformation was particularly important because it facilitated empathetic understanding of the subjects' world of meaning. Kracke explains:

My involvement in treatment of the children completed the undermining of my (defensively) structured research, and initiated the period in which I was most receptive to the concerns of the people I was living with, gathering information on what was their central concern of the moment . . . ," [1985, p. 18].

Police provide an interesting example of the intrapsychic conflicts which can be evoked when a researcher assumes insider status because their role is complex and contradictory. They are rescuers, peacekeepers, and crimefighters. At the same time that they save lives, they also take them away. Ironically, these two facets of the police role are not easily separable, and the act of saving one life may involve destroying another. As many researchers have noted, violence is at the core of the police mandate. The gun is the symbol of their role (Bittner, 1980; Hunt, 1985; Manning, 1980).

Researchers who identify with police and assume membership roles in their culture will have superior access to its informal dimensions (Van Maanen, 1978, 1982; Rubinstein, 1973; Hunt, 1985; Punch, 1978). However, they will also have to deal with the contradictions revolving around the symbolic possession of power which is life-preserving and lethal. Sociological fieldworkers have not routinely collected data which would allow a glimpse into the deeper structure of this contradiction. Nevertheless, a review of the literature reveals that concerns about power and aggression are an essential dimension of the fieldwork encounter in research among police in particular.

John Van Maanen describes the day he was given a Smith and Wesson .357 Magnum by academy classmates. The revolver was the choice street weapon carried by many officers, although departmental regulations forbade its use (Van Maanen, 1982, p. 113). Van Maanen viewed this gift as a mark of his acceptance by police subjects as well as the oddity of his presence in the training class. In another context, he humorously alludes to the illicit dimension of carrying weapons and again notes that it cemented his identification with police. "I was something of a walking talking rule violation, so, too were my colleagues" (Van Maanen, 1988, p. 89). Despite good training and some familiarity, however, Van Maanen remained rather skittish and slightly fearful of guns, a fact that testifies to the intrapsychic conflict that their possession mobilized (Van Maanen, 1988, p. 111).

Similarly, I enjoyed shooting guns but was an incompetent marksperson, a fact which testifies to the existence of unconscious conflict about the weapon rather than an innate skill deficiency (Hunt, 1984). Good pistol shooting involves little else but steady hands and concentration. My ambivalence about power was also revealed in the dream previously cited. In that case, I dealt with guilt about aggression by unloading the gun I am given, making the grips too small, and generally arranging my incompetence at killing even for self-protection.

Although Maurice Punch did not carry a revolver in his fieldwork, he also mentions conflictual feelings which surrounded involvement with guns. For example, when he was asked to hold a gun by a police officer who was busy handcuffing a prisoner, he felt "somewhat foolish as I stood gingerly holding a pistol in the middle of the street while onlookers stared dumbly at the arrest" (Punch, 1978, p. 321). More recently, Punch has used the gun as a metaphor to capture the element of surprise and spontaneity in fieldwork. He comments, "How to cope with a loaded revolver dropped on your lap is something you have to resolve on the spot . . . ." (Punch, 1986, p. 13). In this context, the gun in the lap may refer to the explosiveness of the fieldwork encounter and the emotions that may arise in both subject and researcher.

It should be noted that Punch's symbolism may be gender-specific. It could allude to anxieties about castration and homosexuality, which are mobilized for male researchers in particular. Thus, it is possible that the policeman's gun was placed too close to the researcher's own genitals to allow a margin of comfort. In contrast, as a woman researcher, I was not taken aback when officers unexpectedly handed me a gun or placed one on my lap (Hunt, 1984). I did, however, faint after a plainclothes officer put his revolver in my purse. While eating at a diner, the plainclothes officer requested that I hold the revolver in order to avoid the possibility that someone would call the police and complain of a man with a gun. As neither the food nor my physical health appeared to account for my unusual reaction, I can only surmise that the meaning of having a lethal weapon in my purse was unconsciously problematic.[2]

Police cars represent another metaphor for power, and a researcher's behavior around them may reveal hidden conflicts and ambivalent identifications. John Van Maanen provides an amusing example of the travesties that can result from the conflictual possession of patrol power. The tale involves a number of happenings surrounding the pursuit of a criminal. At some point, Van Maanen is instructed to drive the police car. He explains, "I start the car . . . the lights and siren, to my astonishment, somehow come on. The demonic shotgun is no longer secure and bounces around the front seat, the power brakes feel awkward and almost toss me through the windscreen at the first stop sign. To complicate things, I have no idea of where I'm going." At this point, the passenger door of the car opens, and the equipment begins to tumble out. Van Maanen explains, "The shotgun would have gone too had I not grasped the stock of the weapon with a last-second, panic stricken

lunge. Shamefully, I pull to the side of the road to gather up my litter"
(1988, pp. 113-114).

These fieldwork accounts all reveal various researchers' behavioral
responses to the conflict generated in the face of assuming membership
roles in fieldwork among police. In the absence of each individual's
associations and further knowledge of his or her past, it is not possible
to understand the precise referents. However, derivatives of oedipal
anxieties about the possession of lethal power and defenses against
them seem to be salient in most cases cited. Van Maanen's fieldwork
tale is particularly interesting because it is a creative construction. As
a result, unconscious derivatives, woven between the lines, are more
clearly evident than in the typical scientific account which omits consideration of the affective dimensions of the fieldwork encounter. The
tale also involves a mishap. From a psychoanalytic point of view, a
mishap is similar to the slips of the tongue, mistakes, omissions, and
memory lapses which Freud (1901) grouped in the category of the
psychopathology of everyday life. Although rational factors contribute
to these phenomena, they also usually demonstrate unconscious intent.

In order to develop an understanding of the latent structure of Van
Maanen's mishap, it would be necessary to gather his associations.
However, even in their absence, themes are evident which reflect some
typical unconscious wishes and defenses. In fact, the readers' collective
ability to identify with the fieldworker's predicament at both deep and
surface levels is partly what makes the tale enthralling. We can begin
our analysis with the obvious notation that Van Maanen was uncomfortable in the driver's seat of the patrol car. His discomfort could have
many roots. He may not like driving cars. He could be a poor driver. He
may prefer driving a car with a clutch and be uncomfortable with power
brakes. Police cars contain a myriad of mysterious gadgets that could
evoke fear as well as curiosity in the uninitiated. While there are clearly
many rational explanations for Van Maanen's discomfort, irrational
factors appear to have intensified his confusion and contributed to the
chaos that resulted.

These unconscious factors seem to revolve around oedipal issues in
particular. In fact, it appears likely that Van Maanen suffered a similar
predicament to the one Waud Kracke describes when subjects requested
he assume the authoritative position of doctor in his fieldwork in Brazil.
In order to defend himself against a frightening oedipal victory, Kracke
constructed a dream in which he was ill-equipped to play the role of
Romeo. Symbolically he made himself impotent (Kracke, 1985, pp. 18-

19). In essence, Van Maanen accomplished a similar feat by losing control of key police equipment and allowing the sirens to run amok. Even the shotgun rolled around on the floor, although he saved it from falling out of the car at the last minute. The litter Van Maanen shamefully deposited on the street can also be interpreted as a regressive response to the oedipal anxieties situationally mobilized in the fieldwork encounter.

The above depictions of fieldworker behaviors have been interpreted in terms of the intrapsychic conflict they appear to demonstrate. I have argued that the roles that researchers assume in fieldwork often mobilize transferences as a result of their link to unconscious fantasies. In fieldwork among police, oedipal conflicts and concerns about aggression appear to be a particularly important dimension of the fieldwork encounter for many researchers. The relationship between researchers' conflicts about their identification with police, the transferences mobilized, field relations, and the kind of data gathered is difficult to determine. For reasons that cannot be developed here, sociologists tend to be skeptical about psychoanalysis and often omit consideration of intrapsychic processes, preferring instead to focus on the social and interactional dimensions of behavior.

However, in view of the oedipal conflicts which appear to be universally mobilized in the fieldwork encounter of even the most skilled police researchers, it seems reasonable to speculate about the contribution of these conflicts to one blindspot that appears to haunt much of their work. It is curious that only female fieldworkers appear to have gathered data from female informants to use in general discussions of police culture. (Hunt, 1984; Hunt and Manning, in press). The inclusion of women police adds a richness to the description of police activities absent in the ethnographies of male researchers, who seem to only cultivate male informants. These works by women researchers also avoid the typical distortion of writing accounts of occupational worlds as if no female members exist.

There are certainly a number of rational explanations which could account for most male researchers' blindness to the world of women police. Women are relatively new to the ranks of uniformed patrol, although they have long been involved in detective, undercover, decoy, and juvenile work in many police departments. For example, Van Maanen's first period of fieldwork took place in a police department in which women were not yet admitted to uniformed patrol. As a result, it was easy to omit them from subsequent research samples because they were not among his original informants.

However, even the most rational-appearing decisions in research can have an irrational component. Feminist scholars have long argued that the absence of women from sociological and historical studies of culture is structured by the sexual bias of men who view women and their work as insignificant and unworthy of serious investigation. This omission has generally been corrected in the social science literature, although most of the relevant studies have been done by women.

Although sexism certainly plays a part in some men's blindness to women subjects, there are additional factors which structure this omission. If we deconstruct the surface category of mysogyny and examine the unconscious fantasies from which it is constituted, new light can be shed on the matter. In the case of male researchers doing police field-work, it is possible that blindness to women officers represents a means to defend against oedipal anxieties that are generated in that setting in particular. As father figures, police are hardly benevolent. To the contrary, they are harsh dispensers of justice (and injustice) who have the means to do great harm. For some male researchers, the unconscious significance of the police as paternal transference figures may contribute to fears of oedipal victory and consequent punishment. Researchers may also be attracted to the role of police research because of the romantic appeal of the rescue motif. Unconsciously, rescue fantasies often have oedipal implications. For example, a man's wish to rescue the "fallen women" is sometimes rooted in a desire to save the mother from sexual activity with the father. In this fantasy constellation, the father is often the object of aggression, and the act of rescue implies an oedipal victory for the son. As a result, rescue activities and the fantasies which underlie them may mobilize castration fears as punishment. The fact that police researchers are often exposed to injury and death may also exacerbate their castration concerns.

With this in mind, it can be seen that any activity which heightens the possibility of oedipal victory in the context of research among police becomes doubly problematic. Developing empathetic relationships with policewomen key informants could be unconsciously equated with just such an oedipal conquest. This is the case because policewomen, in contrast to other categories of females, are members of the "police family" and are, therefore, invested with incestuous transference meanings. Some male researchers may respond to the oedipal dilemmas which arise in their work among police by maintaining distance from women and retreating to a regressive identification with policemen. In this setting, at least, a negative oedipal solution is less risky than a symbolic enactment of a positive oedipal fantasy. Blindness to women police, then, constitutes one way to avoid the risks unconsciously linked to oedipal victory. The omission of women in research accounts is multidetermined. Fear of authoritative women of ambiguous gender is another concern that may also be salient for some researchers.

EXPOSURE TO DEATH IMAGES

The fieldworker's exposure to images involving injury, illness, and death often evoke anxiety, in part because they link to deeply rooted wishes and fears. As a result, researchers are likely to erect defenses which help protect them against potentially overwhelming emotional reactions (Devereux, 1967). It should be noted that the sense of danger may not be consciously felt by the researcher. Rather, it is often experienced in the form of a signal which alerts the individual that protective measures are necessary.

My reactions to an experience which occurred in my fieldwork among police illustrates some of the defenses that may be evoked and how they can structure field interactions and observations. I witnessed a horrifying incident in which a woman was stuck under the wheels of a bus. She was screaming for at least thirty minutes while officers attempted to jack up the bus and pull her out. Soon after the bloody incident, I developed a hunger for the spearmint drops which lay on the sergeant's desk.

My desire for food represented one regressive response to the anxiety mobilized in the face of the injured woman. Denial was also extensively employed. Although I was present during the entire rescue operation, I could not remember whether the woman's leg was left severed under the bus when she was put in the ambulance. During the long period in which I was standing around watching the rescue, my memory was also impaired and subsequent note taking difficult. The most detailed notations recorded at the scene involved a surrealistic account of a boy riding a skateboard in the silent street while firemen hosed off the blood. I suspect that my retreat into "the irrelevant" facilitated further denial of what I had witnessed.

During the incident, I tried to be as active as possible and do whatever police instructed to facilitate the rescue. This reached a

50

certain absurdity when I ran rather than walked a block to deliver an unimportant message. While it was culturally syntonic and appropriate to the situation at hand, I suspect my desire to be active served defensive purposes. It protected me against a passive identification with the victim.

Finally, I managed to distance myself from the situation by the use of depersonalization. I was not aware of feeling anxious during the actual incident, although the women's screams were chilling. At the time, my hardness frightened me because I did not think I was responding in a way appropriate to a real human being. As it turned out, my reaction was delayed. While running my usual mile the following morning, I stopped at the corner to let a bus pass before crossing the street. I felt suddenly anxious and was concerned that I would slip beneath the wheels. The woman's screams and her image appeared vividly in my mind.

Exposures to death images create anxiety and necessitate the mobilization of defenses because of the complex fantasies to which they link. In the case of the accident victim, for example, she may have represented myself, as the one who was hurt. At the same time, she was possibly my sister or my mother, two likely archaic victims of aggressive wishes surrounding the oedipal period in particular. Along these lines, it is interesting to note that I distorted the age of the victim in my fieldnotes. Although I could clearly see the victim's face and figure, I perceived her as at least thirty years younger than her sixty years. I suspect that the distortion of the data was structured by transferences. It condensed my own unconscious identification with the victim and a childhood wish that the victim was my rival older sister. Finally, the distortion of age could have represented a defense against aggressive wishes towards my mother. By avoiding recognition that the woman was about her age, I denied the possibility that I could ever wish her harm.

Such unconscious fantasies could account for my irrational anxiety when I was asked to move a police car a block in order to clear the way for a rescue vehicle. At the time, I was dimly aware of a fear that I would wreck the car or wouldn't be able to parallel park. The simple act of driving may have unconsciously represented the enactment of an aggressive fantasy which was intolerable in view of the woman's plight.

Maurice Punch describes similar complex feelings mobilized in the face of his exposure to a homicide during his fieldwork among police. He observed the dead body of a woman stabbed repeatedly by her husband. He also was present when a police officer informed one of the couple's children that her mother was dead. When Punch and the police returned to the precinct, they looked through the keyhole and observed the murderer. Punch notes that he seemed "quite ordinary" (Punch, 1986, p. 310). Punch then returned home, slept several hours, and upon waking, vomited.

It is not uncommon that people respond to stressful situations by getting sleepy. Certainly physical illness and vomiting present clear indications that powerful emotions have been mobilized. In Punch's case, the act of throwing up may have represented a way of getting rid of the truth that he unwittingly swallowed or devoured with his eyes. At a deeper level, the vomiting could have been a reaction to an unconscious childhood fantasy in which the researcher himself committed the heinous deed. If an "ordinary man" could murder his wife, then where does that leave the ordinary researcher?

A detailed examination of the defenses researchers use to deal with exposure to death images in fieldwork is useful in a number of ways. Although, the transferences that underlie defense formation may be idiosyncratic, the specific reactions often are not. Reinharz (1984), for example, describes how her own reactions to wartime shelling in fieldwork in Israel provided valuable data regarding how cultural members handled the stress and strains of war. Similarly, my reactions to the incident with the injured woman shed light on the ways in which police themselves handle exposure to death images. I was not the only witness to the accident who demonstrated anxieties about bodily integrity. For example, when I asked the sergeant if the woman's leg was left severed, he informed me that many policemen also were confused about the status of her leg. Similarly, a number of the police officers experienced amnesia about the details of the event. My partner was assigned the paperwork on the accident because she was first on the scene. She felt alarmed at the prospect of writing the report and requested my help because she could "remember nothing." With the aid of the police Accident Investigation Unit and the sergeant, we were able to piece together an official account which bore some resemblance to the actual incident. A number of policemen also responded to the death image by developing an appetite for food or drink. Others had a reaction similar to that of Maurice Punch and experienced physical illness. Finally, turning passive into active is also a typical way that police handle exposures to these kinds of anxiety-producing images. Although gallows humor is frequently used by police to manage the intrapsychic and social tensions of encounters with injury and death, no police officer was observed to joke during or after this incident.

Knowledge about the researcher's response to exposure to death images in fieldwork is also important because it has implications for relations with subjects and data gathering. In the incident involving the bus accident, for example, I was blinded to certain kinds of data, including the age of the victim. More important observations were also probably omitted from my fieldnotes as a result of perceptual distortions. On the other hand, some of the transferences and defenses that were mobilized may have had positive implications for rapport. My awareness of my own regressive response attuned me to those of the police and facilitated a peculiar kind of empathy. Thus, although I felt embarrassed that I was hungry after such a horrible scene, my hunger lead me to be sensitive to the possible needs of police. As a result, I was quick to offer comfort to a sergeant who had bravely suspended his emotions of help his troops through the ordeal. I told him gently that *he* looked pale and tired and then suggested that it might help a bit if he went home and had a glass of scotch. Although I neither drank scotch myself or knew his preferences, my suggestion was not entirely random. I associated scotch to a mixed drink called a Cadillac which combines milk and whiskey. I unconsciously offered the officer a food which combined the maternal nurturance I needed with the masculine imagery that would make it palatable to him.

THE UNCONSCIOUS DYNAMICS OF COLLECTING DATA

Numerous researchers have noted the discomfort and guilt which occasionally accompany the research task. Most accounts connect these feelings to the ambiguities of the fieldworker's role as part spy, part voyeur, and part cultural member. Few, however, have been explicit as to why these roles should engender guilt. In fact, it may not be simply the roles that evoke discomfort but the process of doing research itself. Thus, unconscious fantasies may not only mediate the encounter with another culture, exposure to death images, and the roles that researchers play, they may also bear on the process of sociological inquiry. Asking questions, making observations, listening to conversations, and doing structured and unstructured interviews may mobilize transferences. The inner conflicts evoked in the data-gathering process are managed by each researcher in different ways. Fieldworkers who find interviewing problematic, for example, may avoid the conflictual techniques, omit questions that seem particularly ominous, or limit the inquiry to exclude those categories of people who present the most difficulty.

This structuring of conversational and interview data is often subtle and not easy to detect. Researchers may simply "forget" to ask certain questions of certain people. They may ask the relevant question but not really hear the answer. They may launch their inquiry in a manner which is unempathetic and limits the responses received. They may be more attuned to one person's answers than to another's. Researchers may also simply not think to ask certain kinds of questions. Others may avoid a question and justify the decision on rational and instrumental grounds. Regardless of the reasons and justifications, unintended distortions are often introduced into the process of data collection as a result.

The mobilization of transferences surrounding the process of inquiry may go beyond a particular question. Gathering any sort of data may assume unconscious meanings. The fantasies which can mediate the process of sociological inquiry are multiple and vary with the individual researcher. For example, a female researcher may view gathering data from men as an act of emasculation (stealing his secrets/his valuables/his jewels) and experience guilt. The process of inquiry may also be linked to fears of doing harm by exposing research subjects to danger. For example, after discovering some key data from a male informant, one woman researcher whom I interviewed had a dream which involved stealing clothes. One theme that dominated her associations involved a fantasy in which gathering data was equated with stripping loved ones of protective gear and exposing them to hostile elements. As the researcher cared deeply for her research subjects as both friends and transference objects, she did not consciously want to do them harm. As a result, images of self-punishment were also present in the dream and her associations to it.

Male researchers may develop complementary conflicts about gathering data from women. For example, asking questions may be viewed as an interrogation, unconsciously associated to a sadistic sexual act with an incestuous object. Alternatively, developing empathetic relations with female informants may be viewed as an unconscious oedipal victory which brings with it the threat of injury which must be defended against.

One woman researcher engaged in a study of South American Indians shared a dream with me which provides a specimen demonstrating some of the typical unconscious dynamics which may be evoked in the data gathering process. Every dream condenses multiple meanings, and only a full account of the dreamer's associations in the context of the psychoanalytic situation would enable us to decode the script and discover the rich texture of unconscious fantasy woven between the lines. Nevertheless, the associations the researcher does provide reveal that oedipal conflicts were dominant.

The researcher begins her narrative by describing the cultural context in which the dream took place. She goes on to relate the dream and additional associations to it. Note that she first thought this second trip to the Amazon occurred nine months after the first. She then checks the dates in her log and corrects herself. This error may relate to the oedipal themes which emerge in the dream text and associations. Thus, an unconscious pregnancy fantasy may lie at the heart of her desire to study primitive fertility practices.

> The second sequel of dreams took place some nine months after my first visit to the Amazon. No let me check, it was seven months. I went to (the capital), three days ahead of my friends to meet Silvia, an older woman who was supposed to introduce me to the healer. I was interested in studying infertility and thought he would be a good source of information about herbal medicine. Silvia is a married, upper class-woman, from one of the ruling families in the country. But, she confided in me that her marriage was not happy. We stayed in her house, as a result of a curfew. It was part of a beautiful compound with wrought iron gates, vegetation and flowers. When I went out to dinner with Silvia and her daughter, Silvia warned me not to wear my gold bracelet because thieves were everywhere. "Don't put your jewels in your purse," she said. We talked about a number of issues, including her occupation and life style but put politics aside because the political situation in the country was tumultuous. That night I had the following dream. I'm sleeping in a hotel room and awaken. My aunt is there. She's my mother's younger sister and is four years older than me. Sarah is taking care of the children and cooking. Another girl comes in the room. We all have an appointment with the priest-healer. I am very angry at this girl because she is not contributing anything. When I awake in the dream everything is gone, the alarm clock . . . my valuables. I think that my mother warned me and I feel totally invaded and angry. I think, "you take whatever you want without regard for me."

> My thoughts about the dream? I am aware I felt angry and jealous of the idle, rich women, like Silvia. They can take whatever they want. Silvia reminded me a lot of my mother. They are both very petite women. Silvia's house was like my mother's, elegant, charming, and beautiful. What Silvia said about the bracelet, the jewelry, was just like something that my

mother would say. "Don't wear your jewelry, don't put jewelry in your
purse." It was like telling me not to let men know how attractive I am.
"Don't let a man put his jewels in your purse. Don't show off your
jewelry." I think that I was sort of my mother's boy when I was a girl. She
wanted me as her son, certainly not a competitor! She even took away my
dolls when I was little! When I had gone to Silvia's home, she had shown
me her husband's room which had a lot of black leather furniture. I
remember this beautiful leather winged chair. I just ran in and sat on it!
Her house was so familiar. It was so much like mine. My father and I were
very close. I think he wanted a son, too. So I was his son and also his
mistress, his secret lover.

I have a number of thoughts about my guilt in relation to asking Silvia
questions. She had confided in me her problems about her husband. My
own parents always seemed on the edge of divorce. And there was
something else too. Silvia and I had gone to the healing priest together.
She was multilingual and well-educated. I could not speak much of the
native language, so she helped translate my questions to the priest and his
answers to me. I told the priest that I was studying human sexuality and
was interested in questions of infertility. He knew what I was asking and
told me about the cures for impotence among the natives. I felt guilty
because Silvia was translating all of this sexual material. It was in
scientific language but it was, nevertheless, still sexual. I thought I was
not protecting her. She seemed like such a sheltered creature.

The dream and associations make clear that the informant, Silvia,
was the object of a complex maternal transference. The wealthy woman
resembles the dreamer's mother in looks, taste, and life-style. The
woman's luxurious dwelling feels intimately familiar to the researcher
because it resembles her mother's own home. Silvia's warning that the
researcher avoid displaying her jewels and keep them out of her purse
is unconsciously linked to similar prohibitions by her mother. Thus, the
researcher interprets the woman's advice as an effort to squelch her
feminine sexuality. In this context, she notes that her own mother
avoided experiencing her daughter as a competitive threat by treating
her as if she were a boy and taking away her dolls when she was a child.
The oedipal rivalry between Silvia and the researcher is reenacted when
the researcher is shown the husband's room and jumps into his winged
chair. In this gesture, she symbolically slips into the arms of her father
and displaces the mother.

The researcher's guilt about asking questions relates to several dimensions of the unconscious oedipal scenario that mediated the fieldwork encounter. Consciously, the researcher is uncomfortable about asking questions concerning occupation and life-style. She also feels that she has inadvertently exposed this sheltered woman to sexuality when she requests that she translate the conversation with the priest-healer. Her dreams and associations reveal the deeper roots of her guilt about collecting data. Thus, there is an oedipal triangle in each dream sequence and its associations. First, we see the researcher in the home of the woman and her husband. The woman has shared with the researcher the fact that she is disappointed in her marriage. The dreamer recalls the occasion in which she was shown the husband's special room and sat in his chair. A second triadic encounter involves the wealthy woman, the researcher, and the priest. In this case, the researcher also has privileged sexual knowledge. This time it comes indirectly from Silvia who translates the words of the priest-healer. The priest could be viewed as a paternal transference figure, like Silvia's husband. In this instance, Silvia acts as the conduit to the sexual communications between father and daughter. She has not been protected from either the daughter's desire or the father's seduction. It is, therefore, not just any sexual knowledge from which Silvia is insufficiently protected, but the researcher's wish to share intimacies with a father figure who does not belong to her.

The fact that Silvia shared intimate information about her marital difficulties with the researcher may have helped to mobilize the latter's guilt. Thus, we learn that the researcher's own parents were periodically on the verge of divorce. The researcher, therefore, grew up in a family situation in which oedipal victory was ever too possible and therefore unbearably risky. This knowledge helps us to understand another dimension of the researcher's desire to sit in the husband's winged chair. Not only does the act symbolize desire to have the father but also to take his place and be the man. By being a boy, the little girl protects herself against the fulfillment of dangerous oedipal wishes. Along these lines, the researcher notes that her father wanted a boy as a child and that she was both his mistress and his son.

In summary, this dream provides a case study which shows a relationship between the process of sociological inquiry and the mobilization of transferences. I suspect that gathering information, stealing, and oedipal victory, are just a few of the common unconscious fantasies that may mediate the technical aspects of the research endeavor. Whatever the particular fantasy mobilized, its management can have an important effect on the data-gathering process. Some researchers may handle feelings of envy and guilt by avoiding close relations with those subjects who mobilize uncomfortable feelings. On occasion, unconscious fantasies may be enacted which do not serve the interests of the research enterprise. For example, researchers may unintentionally behave toward certain subjects in a distant, angry, cold, or provocative manner which resembles the way they acted towards significant others in childhood. As a result, rapport may be undermined and data limited. Researchers may also engage in sexualized encounters with subjects who are the object of transferences or associated with them. On occasion, these encounters may structure field relations in problematic ways and even threaten the psychological welfare of the researcher.

Male and female researchers may avoid asking questions of opposite sex subjects or cultivating them as informants if guilty fantasies link to this endeavor. In some cases, the researcher's actions can be rationally justified by social factors. For example, it has often been suggested that researchers have better access to same-sex informants. Although this may be true in some cultural settings in which there is a rigid division between male and female domains, the researcher's transferences may also play a role in the decision to segregate the collection of data. Whatever the specifics of the fantasy, future researchers would do well to examine these processes in detail in order to minimize the way unconscious factors interfere with their research and maximize their understanding of the unconscious structuring of the research enterprise.

4. TRANSFERENCE AND COUNTERTRANSFERENCE IN FIELDWORK

As researchers become immersed in the field, they develop different kinds of relationships with research subjects. The close ties which emerge in the relationship between researcher and key informant are particularly conducive to the mobilization of transference. Thus, both researcher and subject routinely impose archaic images onto the person of the other. Sometimes the transferences develop independently. At others, those of the researcher and subject are related in complementary or reciprocal ways. The unconscious images that mediate relations between researcher and subject are particularly important to examine. At the most obvious level, they affect rapport. Researchers' transferences may result in inappropriate behaviors which impede empathetic relationships with subjects or blind researchers to important parts of subjects' reality. In some cases, relationships with key informants may even be terminated (LeVine, 1981). In most cases, transferences simply define the relationship in particular ways. In interviews with subjects with whom the researcher has good rapport, transferences may emerge which structure the questions asked, the answers heard, and, ultimately, the materials collected as data. Methodological as well as perceptual defenses may be instituted to distance the researcher from data which arouses anxiety as a result of its link to conflictual past memories.

In the clinical setting, the term transference generally refers to the unconscious, archaic images that the patient imposes on the analyst. Countertransference is defined as the unconscious reaction of the analyst to the patient, significant people in the patient's life, his or her ideation, and transference. The fieldwork encounter is complex, and the terms transference and countertransference are not directly translatable to the researcher-subject interaction. Fieldwork does not take place in the laboratory-like environment of the psychoanalyst's office. It is heavily mediated by cultural factors and the real role the researcher plays in the subject's life. As a result, it is sometimes difficult to differentiate the transferences which arise from the researcher's unconscious, independent of the subject's, and those which emerge in relation to the subject's transferences. In order to avoid confusion in the discussion of transference and countertransference in fieldwork, narrow definitions will be utilized.

The term transference will be used to refer to researchers' unconscious reactions to the subjects and some aspect of their world. Transference will also be used to describe the unconscious archaic images that the subject imposes onto the person of the researcher. Countertransference, in contrast, will be used to refer to the researcher's unconscious reaction to the subject's transference. In most cases, the unconscious world of the subject is ambiguous. As a result, the term countertransference will be used sparingly. Before going on to examine cases of transference and countertransference in fieldwork, a review of selected psychoanalytic writings on the subject is in order.

The Clinical Setting

Early in his work with patients, Freud discovered the phenomenon of transference. He learned that patients often did not perceive the doctor in terms of the way he actually felt or presented himself. Instead, they routinely attributed to him emotional attitudes and characteristics which belonged to significant others from their past. Initially, Freud believed that these transferences presented an obstacle to therapeutic treatment. He later revised this view, noting that the analysis of the patients' transference provided a key to understanding the past.

Freud discovered the phenomenon of countertransference soon after he became aware of transference. Physicians, regardless of their personal health, integrity, and commitment to cure sometimes experienced transference reactions to the patient. The physician's unconscious reactions to the patient's transferences were termed countertransferences. Freud viewed countertransferences as an impediment to empathetic understanding because they blinded the analyst to the meaning of the patient's materials. He therefore recommended that physicians undergo a didactic analysis as part of their formal training, in order to rid themselves of problematic neurotic conflicts.

Some psychoanalysts have broadened the definition of countertransference to take account of the entire set of reactions that an analyst may have to some aspect of the patient, his or her transference, objects, or ideation which influences the analyst's understanding and technique (Little, 1951; Heimann, 1950; Searles, 1979). From this point of view, countertransference is viewed as universal and inevitable. While it sometimes seems to interfere with the smooth course of an analysis, it is part of the process to be harnessed into promoting analytic understanding. Other analysts find such broad definitions of countertransference problematic because they confuse empathy and other conflict-free modes of understanding with those that are pathological. The latter focus on the reactions that link to neurotically tinged conflicts in the analyst, revived by the patient's material, which blind the analyst to the patient's inner world (Silverman, 1985; Kern, 1978; Blum, 1986). From this perspective, it is the successful analysis of the countertransference reaction which deepens understanding rather than merely its experience.

The case of Anna O. provides the classic example of a transference-countertransference dynamic that developed between a patient and doctor who did not have the benefit of undergoing psychoanalytic treatment. Anna O. was a female patient of Freud's colleague Breuer. She was being treated for hysteria with a combination of hypnosis and the cathartic method. At this historical juncture, psychoanalysis had not yet been discovered, and therapists were neither encouraging free association nor using interpretation as the method of cure. As it turned out, Breuer developed a special interest in his attractive, young patient and talked about her incessantly to his wife. His wife became jealous and manifested this in morose and unhappy moods. Concerned about his wife's unhappiness and frightened by his feelings for his patient, Anna O., Breuer suddenly decided to terminate treatment. That night, he was called to Anna O.'s bed, only to discover that his patient was in the middle of an hysterical pregnancy. Breuer tried to calm her and then fled the house. He and his wife then went on a second honeymoon. This resulted in the birth of a child who committed suicide many years later (Jones, 1961). In this case, Breuer developed an erotic countertransference in response to his patient's transference love for him. He was not able to fully examine his feelings towards his patient nor hers for him. As a result, the feelings and the fantasies to which they linked remained largely unconscious and were therefore enacted by both. Anna O. developed a false pregnancy in which Breuer was the fantasied father. Breuer abruptly ended treatment and conceived a baby with his wife. In doing so, he defended himself against his desires for Anna O. and, at the same time, allowed the symbolic fulfillment of them.

Hate can also appear in the countertransference and interfere with analytic understanding and technique (Winnicott, 1949). In one case, a candidate at an urban psychoanalytic institute was referred a patient by a prominent senior analyst. The candidate soon discovered that the patient was plagued with a foot fetish, a symptom that does not portend favorably for successful psychoanalytic treatment, although other therapies may be helpful. Apparently, the patient had kept this fact hidden in his initial consultation with the senior analyst who had assured the candidate the patient was analyzable.

The man was an extremely difficult patient. He frequently missed appointments, claiming that professional obligations were more important than his analytic hour. More grating were the chronic, intense hostility and rage he displayed towards the psychiatrist. The latter's difficulty was complicated by the fact that the patient was a training case. The successful completion of the analysis could have bearing on the timing of the psychiatrist's certification by the American Psychoanalytic Association. The fact that the patient was referred by a senior analyst and possible father competitor probably heightened the intensity of the countertransference. Indeed, one can put oneself in the doctor's shoes and recognize that this patient might well be experienced as a highly ambivalent "gift."

The candidate's emerging countertransference reaction made itself undeniably apparent in an incident which occurred immediately before the patient's hour. The candidate decided to change the lights above the couch and, upon reaching the ceiling, accidentally broke the bulbs. Glass shattered onto the couch where the troublesome patient would soon rest. At this point, the candidate could no longer avoid recognition of his rage. He picked up the glass from the couch and, one imagines, himself lay down for some self-analysis before proceeding to the next hour. It should be noted that in the psychoanalytic situation, as well as in fieldwork and everyday life, transferences and countertransferences are usually subtle and far more resistant to detection than the two examples cited above (Kern, 1978; Jacobs, 1986).

The Fieldwork Setting

Transference reactions that emerge in fieldwork and clinical settings are similar in kind. However, the fieldworker's immersion in the real-life world of subjects complicates their detection. This is the case when the affective and behavioral responses in which the transferences are embedded seem appropriate to the social context. The researcher who is repeatedly harassed by rude and rejecting subjects is bound to feel angry, hurt, and upset. Similarly, researchers who find themselves in a car chase or knife fight or who watch someone die painfully may experience extreme reactions which are situationally justified. In contrast to the analyst, the researcher develops friendships with subjects. These cannot be exclusively subsumed within a psychodynamic category. Unfortunately, however, the recognition that situational realities and "real" relationships are a fundamental feature of the research encounter has too often led to the omission of intrapsychic issues altogether. Thus, the researcher's reactions to any encounter may well be situationally derived and reality-based but nevertheless mobilize intrapsychic conflict.

The same clues that psychoanalysts employ to help them recognize countertransference in the analytic setting may be used by the researcher. Strong emotions of anger, anxiety, love or shame, boredom, or annoyance may all indicate the presence of transferences. Jean Briggs (1970, 1987), for example, explicitly used the appearance of feelings like annoyance as a fieldwork tool. She assumed they indicated a transference block which impeded empathy. Rather than avoid examination of materials which aroused such feelings, she made them objects of inquiry. Reactions that seem inappropriate or peculiar in social context may also suggest that defenses are at work to ward off transference-generated anxiety. The latter is particularly true in native versus cross-cultural fieldwork. However, it should be noted that transferences are also sometimes subtly disguised beneath ordinary scientific methodologies and neutral "good person" behaviors and feelings (Jacobs, 1986; Devereux, 1967). The analysis of dreams, fantasies, parapraxes, jokes, and other symbolic expressions provides a particularly useful way to explore the dynamics of the researcher's transference. These images and the researcher's associations to them often provide direct links to the unconscious thoughts which impose themselves on the present. They also provide important data regarding the kinds of unconscious fantasies that are lived out vicariously in the fieldwork endeavor, structure the researcher's role behaviors, and affect relations with subjects.

This discussion of transferences in fieldwork will assume a classical psychoanalytic perspective and focus on their negative impact. However, it should be kept in mind that fieldworkers have also noted that the researcher's transferences to particular key informants may be useful in fieldwork because they facilitate awareness of subtle aspects of the individual and his or her culture which would otherwise go unnoticed. Waud Kracke provides an example from his study of the Kagwahiv Indians. At a time when he was ill with a badly infected foot, he woke up in the night and saw the flickering of a cooking fire. Looking through the crack in the thatch of his wall, he saw his informant Mõhagi warming himself by the fire, singing softly. Kracke had the intense fantasy, amounting to almost a conviction, that Mõhagi was saying spells to insure the healing of his foot. Kracke's fantasy was partly rooted in a maternal transference. He wished for someone to be as solicitous of his health as his mother might be. His perception of Mõhagi also had a core of correctness. It was not long after having this fantasy that Kracke conducted observations and interviews which verified to what degree Mõhagi did, indeed, have an aspiration to be a shamanistic curer. The intense transference reaction provided the first perception of this deep trend in the subject's character and led Kracke to explore this dimension of his personality (Kracke, 1987, p. 73).

The following examples of transference reactions in fieldwork were selected because they involve issues of power, race, gender, and sexuality. Sociologists have traditionally explored such issues as manifestations of cultural conflicts related to ethnocentrism, sexism, or racism.

However, value conflicts often link to key unconscious fantasies in such a way that intrapsychic tensions are increased. As a result, researchers' difficulties handling these conflicts may be greatly exacerbated. The researcher who is able to recognize when transferences mediate cultural conflicts is likely to have an easier time managing them and maintaining good field relations.

EXAMPLE 1: INSIDE THE MEDICAL SETTING

My research in a medical setting mobilized transferences that were detrimental to field relations. I was about to begin observing the inter-actions between doctors and patients in the emergency room of a psychiatric hospital. I wanted to learn some clinical psychiatry and familiarize myself with the social world of medicine. Eventually, I hoped to conduct an in-depth study of psychiatric culture. However, I was experiencing so much anxiety that I was concerned about my ability to go ahead with the project. A number of "rational" explanations for my worry went through my mind. Past research interests had involved the study of relatively powerless groups including peasants and South American Indians. Eventually, I conducted a study of police, a working class group, who, despite the appearance of power, retain a low-status, liminal role in society. They do the dirty work of the ruling elite, mediating between rich and poor, black and white, and husband and wife. In typical sociological tradition, I found it easier to empathize with disenfranchised, marginal persons than those with status, wealth, and power. The medical profession, in particular, was the focus of ambivalence. I shared with women friends many unpleasant encounters with doctors but also knew some kind and competent ones who helped balance the picture. I am also a doctor's daughter, was surrounded by the medical culture in my youth, and am intimately familiar with the peculiar combination of contempt and caring that characterizes the occupational personality of many physicians. Both patients and non-medical co-workers appear subject to their ambivalence. Psychiatrists, for example, even those who have been psychoanalyzed, often display an irrational arrogance when they compare themselves with other mental health professionals.

It occurred to me that the fieldwork situation itself could be the source of anxiety. Medical settings can be particularly difficult in view of their hierarchical organization and the marginal roles attributed to nonmedical people. Although the low-status, stranger role is hardly pleasant, it did not seem to account for the level of anxiety I experienced during this initial period. After all, resistance to the presence of a stranger is hardly unusual in fieldwork. I had previously done fieldwork among police, who are unusually suspicious of outsiders, and did not feel so anxious. I understood that their resistance to my presence was based on fear rather than intentional maliciousness. Like the analysis of resistance for the psychoanalyst clinician, the process of developing trust in fieldwork is fundamental to the endeavor. In my fieldwork among police, at least, I viewed it as an important emotional, intellectual, and behavioral challenge (Hunt, 1984; Adler and Adler, 1987).

After a very uncomfortable few days in the psychiatric emergency room, I was ready to abandon the ship before the voyage began. My anxiety had heightened to the point where it was necessary to maintain aloofness from residents. Eventually, it became evident that rational explanations for worries were inadequate. Irrational transferences were interfering with the work. That evening, I had a dream, the analysis of which led to an insight which greatly reduced my anxiety. My brother-in-law was diapering his baby but did not wash his hands after having completed the task, even though they were soiled. My associations led to a number of incidents which occurred in my fieldwork among police. In one, a policeman approached a drunken, homeless man lying on the street. He had to get him up and walking but wanted to avoid contamination. Eventually, the officer was forced to use his hands to help the drunk. When the situation was resolved, the policeman returned to the patrol car, holding his hands up in the air "like a surgeon entering an operating room."

This last association to the dream provided the link between my present experience at the hospital and the past. I recalled a painful memory of some twelve years ago in which an orthopedic surgeon had threatened to have residents, rather than himself, perform a necessary operation in the very public hospital where I was beginning participant observation. At first, he had agreed to perform the surgery for a reduced fee at a private hospital. I was a student and had no insurance. He then abruptly changed his mind. Suffice it to say that the dream had many more referents. One can imagine that my own analyst ("the brain surgeon") was represented in the script. He had kindly agreed to see me for a lower fee than is typical for persons of his skill and experience.

At a deeper level, it is logical to assume that the anxiety linked to unresolved oedipal fantasies about my father. In fact, he had been the chief resident in the very hospital in which I was currently doing my research. Thus, it appeared that my peculiar status in the emergency room had triggered a regressive response. The closeness to my father was symbolized by working in the field of psychiatry and in his former hospital. My analyst's kind fee arrangement also possibly evoked oedipal conflicts. I responded by retreating into an old fantasy pattern which was much reinforced by my relatively low status in the institution and the immediate presence of others of varying rank. Guilty about a possible oedipal victory, I imagined myself the opposite — punished, weak, and injured — the way I had formerly felt with the surgeon. The theme of sibling rivalry also appeared in the dream and linked to the fieldwork situation. The image of the baby, for example, was possibly associated to the birth of my brother when I was five. At the time, I had also felt displaced and powerless, a feeling which was situationally mobilized during several unpleasant encounters in the hospital setting.[3]

The analysis of the dream, in particular the conscious establishment of a link between my current concern about working in the emergency room and the experience with the surgeon, led to a great reduction in anxiety. I was able to develop good working relationships with several residents and be empathetically attuned to others. An interaction which occurred while I was on the resident's ward partly demonstrated the latter. The chief resident initially refused to help by providing a resident who I could observe interviewing patients, claiming that the patients were too new, too old, or too soon to be transferred. As an experienced fieldworker, it was obvious that the patients were not the issue but the residents. They did not welcome the presence of a stranger, and the "Chief" was trying to protect them. Eventually, pressure was exerted on the "Chief" who then instructed me to follow a young woman just assigned to the ward. As it turned out, the woman was French, and her English was poor. The psychotic patients could not easily understand her and frequently asked me to translate. Despite my efforts to assure the resident that I was there to learn and not to judge, it was clear that the resident was uncomfortable. I empathized with this resident, also a low-caste stranger, and eventually abandoned this part of the project rather than increase her discomfort.

As a result of my analysis of the transference reactions evoked in the medical setting, I was able to handle my own low status more effectively. In particular, I took action which had previously evaded me to facilitate increased cooperation by ward attendings and the chief resident. I could also more easily understand institutional power arrangements without feeling personally injured, and insight into the psychodynamics of power relations inside the medical organization was gained. The attitudes of medical doctors towards Ph.D. psychologists, for example, became the subject of an interesting analysis. These attitudes are partly rooted in the medical doctor's efforts to maintain power and control over scarce resources and also in some legitimate differences in philosophies of training. They also have unconscious roots.[4]

EXAMPLE 2: SEXISM AND TRANSFERENCE

Perhaps the most typical and easily detectable transference responses are those that suddenly disrupt communication in interviews or conversations by experienced and sensitive fieldworkers. Ruth Horowitz, for example, mentions a conversation with a male member of a Chicago youth gang. She was talking to a "lion" whose girlfriend had just told him that she was pregnant. Horowitz explains, "My reporter role got the best of me and I made the mistake of asking why they did not use birth control in a tone that he took as an indictment of his behavior. With that comment what had been a fascinating conversation about his intimate life, his fears of marriage and fatherhood, turned into a discussion of sports and fights." (Horowitz 1986, p. 419)

Although Horowitz attributes this mistake to value conflicts which made it difficult for her to understand why it was taboo for gang members to use birth control, given its normative prevalence in her own cultural milieu, it seems likely that additional factors also structured the lapse in empathy. According to Horowitz, the lion wanted to neither take responsibility for his child nor marry the mother (Horowitz, personal communication). It seemed possible that his irresponsible and callous attitude towards his pregnant girlfriend may have mobilized the researcher's unconscious identification with the girlfriend and her child. This response is similar to what psychoanalysts call a countertransference identification with the patient's "objects," a not infrequent occurrence in the analytic setting as well as in research (Jacobs, 1983). Thus, Horowitz may have unconsciously experienced some resentment towards the boy which surfaced unintentionally in the words that followed his discussion of the pregnancy. Her question was possibly interpreted by the subject as punitive and moralistic, and he responded to the perceived attack by withdrawing defensively. Thus, in a sudden twist in the narrative, he put on his masculine armor and talked about fighting and athletic feats.

EXAMPLE 3: RACISM AND TRANSFERENCE

My own fieldwork among Metro City Police was long-term and intensive. I spent eighteen months doing participant observation on a daily basis. In view of the ideological conflicts that existed between me and my subjects, there were many areas in which empathetic communication was difficult to achieve. Transferences were probably a more pervasive feature of my fieldwork than I would care to note. One particular area that I found politically and personally sensitive was race. Metro City Police displayed a pervasive contempt for the black community, a contempt that was offensive and difficult to ignore. This was apparent in their language as well as behavior. For example, white, lower-class community members were frequently labeled "critters," "toads," and "skells." Blacks were given special names that set them below and apart from whites, such as "deuce" and "nigger." The former term was derived from the police entrance examination in which the respondent checks box one, two, or three, depending on whether his or her ethnicity is white, black, or other. Like the label "nigger," "deuce," is clearly degrading, condensing the meanings of second rate, inferior, and next to nonhuman. Nicknames of black officers and civilians also seemed to display the belief they were atavistic or subhuman. For example, white police named a black officer "Massa" because he allegedly resembled the gorilla in the Metro City Zoo.

Most of the time, I was able to manage my irritation at white police for their racism by remaining silent or asking questions of clarification. This response helped to reduce the tension of the moment and further enlightened me about white police's construction of racial categories. For example, when I first heard a police officer use the term "deuce," I felt annoyed. Recognizing that my reaction indicated both cultural and intrapsychic conflict, I used it as a signal that the topic was worth investigation. I politely inquired how the term was derived and later recorded the answer in my fieldnotes. At other times, I simply pretended to ignore police remarks and often did not record them. This reaction was defensive and did not increase my understanding of police racial attitudes. However, at least it did not undermine friendly relations. The fact that my fieldnotes demonstrate a relative absence of material on race, despite the abundance of data available, does suggest that I cultivated a blindness to manage my own discomfort with the issue. I believe that my difficulty with the racial issues and the related gap in my notes, in part constituted a transference reaction. There was one incident in particular in which the nature of the "racial" transference became evident. In this case, my annoyance with the racist talk of one officer got the better of me and I responded with a cruel retort. As it turned out, his words linked to some disturbing unconscious memories which were symbolically condensed in my verbal response to him.

One evening I was standing outside of the police district, waiting for my partner, when a veteran officer approached and began to chat. The officer's conversation concerned his distaste for blacks and was frequently punctuated by the word "nigger." I began to feel annoyed as I listened but initially refrained from comment. In the middle of his dialogue, however, the officer suddenly interrupted his flow of thought and asked how I got "so tan in just one day at the beach." Without thinking, I responded, "I didn't tell you about my grandmother huh," clearly implying that my grandmother was black. The officer was taken back by my response, said he felt guilty, and asked if it was true. I assured him that it wasn't true. Nevertheless, he changed the topic of conversation and ceased to talk about his racial attitudes. Certainly rapport was disrupted, for the moment at least. Had I been interested in gathering materials about racial issues, for example, I doubt if this officer would have been as open about his views as he was prior to my comment.

Although, I was not immediately aware of what had triggered my response, self-analysis has subsequently revealed some of its unconscious roots. Although I was annoyed by the officer's use of the term "nigger," the link between the present situation and my childhood was activated when he innocently asked about my tan. When I was a child, I spent my summers with my cousins and grandmother in the south. My grandmother was a genteel southern lady, whose kind but paternalistic treatment of blacks was always a source of childhood conflict. It was particularly disturbing in relation to black housekeepers who were important maternal figures with whom I identified. In fact, my southern relatives often pointed out that my tan skin looked negro. Pronounced with a southern accent, the latter word sounded like "nigra," which always seemed uncomfortably close to the racial slur. My angry retort in this fieldwork interaction condensed moral indignation about the racial attitudes of my grandmother as well as the police. It also disguised an "inverted" family romance regarding my own heritage. Typically, children share an unconscious fantasy that their real parents are kings and queens or have some other regal background (Freud, 1909). In contrast, I apparently fantasized that my family heritage was partly black. Thus, at one level, I had not really lied to the officer when I suggested that my tan skin was natural. Indeed, my surrogate mothers had been black housekeepers.[5]

EXAMPLE 5: SEXUAL CONFLICT IN A HOMOSEXUAL SETTING

Transference dilemmas may be particularly acute in fieldwork settings in which the researcher's personal sexual beliefs and practices conflict with those of subjects. Regardless of their ideological commitment to gay rights, for example, few heterosexual men could do fieldwork among homosexuals without experiencing conflict. This is because research subjects openly express childhood fantasies that are repressed in the researcher. Social factors which ordinarily aid repression are absent. As a result, the researcher's defenses are undermined, and unacceptable fantasies may emerge uncomfortably close to consciousness. The result of this is that the researcher experiences the signal of anxiety and automatically mobilizes defenses to help maintain repression. Although these defenses can be personally helpful to the researcher, they can be troublesome to the fieldwork endeavor if they inhibit empathy, enhance distance from subjects, or blind the researcher to important aspects of their world.

The following case study explores some psychodynamic dimensions of a researcher's fieldwork encounter with homosexual police. The researcher is a male heterosexual who is minimally conflicted about his sexuality and gender identity. As a result, his experience provides a particularly good example of the kinds of conflicts which are likely to emerge for most male heterosexual fieldworkers in this setting. Although this fieldwork situation is somewhat unusual, the general psychodynamics are not. Any fieldwork encounter involves a shifting interplay of social interaction, unconscious fantasy, anxiety, and defense. Let us begin the analysis with a summary of three consecutive interviews I conducted with the researcher. These took place during the first few months of fieldwork.

INTERVIEW 1

Did I tell you that I was thinking of retiring [from the police department]. . . . I think it's about time, but I still have some concerns. Things have been getting worse and worse lately . . . my sinuses are a mess . . . then the stock market. I had put a lot of money in mutual funds. It was nice over the summer. We had fun. But the crash came and a lot was lost. . . . Well, let me tell you about the induction [ceremony of the organization for gay officers]. First when I got there, I walked in the wrong door, walked out and then walked back in again. John was there. He ushered me in. I was a little uncomfortable because no one made me feel at ease. But it was just a normal interaction, nothing really happened. There was one thing. I was talking to John, the psychologist, and this other guy comes over and interrupts. He just took John away. I guess he was his lover or something and maybe he got jealous. It annoyed me a little . . . I mean I thought I had found somebody who was really interesting and not threatening. It was business. We were talking about my book, just having a discussion. . . . I had wanted to bring my wife, as a security blanket, something to fall back on. I would have shied away from her, no dancing or anything. But it would have made things easier. . . . But generally, you wouldn't know that it was any different from any other gathering. It was like my interview with Gary (another homosexual). He was on T.V. and looked normal, you know straight. We planned to meet for drinks and I told him what I had on and he told me what he had on, so we could recognize each other. We sat at the bar and talked. Everything was ordinary. We had a few drinks. Then, suddenly, you know, he just began to swish. Thank God I had Kathy [my wife] with me. . . . Anyway, it was like that at the ceremony. I walked into the room and not much was going on, nothing unusual. Then, all of a sudden it just degenerated [laughs, astonished]. The men began to dance together, had their hands in their pockets, in each other's pants, on their asses! I don't think that would happen at a straight party. . . . I'm worried about the book. I got this note from this other psychologist who is also writing a book. He must have been upset by my participation in the meeting. I think that the problem is that there are some people there who are not yet out of the closet. They don't trust anyone and are worried about betrayal. It's almost paranoid. . . . I've not asked any of their names. What are you doing with those notes? Can I have a copy?

. . . Oh, yes, the orange vodka. I was worried about getting AIDS and I noticed that they were all changing drinks. Someone would get up and dance and someone else would take his drink. I started out with a drink with lime in it. Then I switched to vodka and orange. This way I could make sure whose it was and no one would take it. I also clutched the drink like this [the researcher puts his hand around an imaginary glass and moves his hand up and down]. I don't recall holding onto a glass like that at any other party! That was unusual. There were two psychologists there and I wonder if they noticed my behavior. I wonder what they would say? I'm not sure if I could tell them about it. . . .

INTERVIEW 2 (ONE WEEK LATER)

I just sold my stock and that took a load off my mind. . . . Well, I did it. I'm [a member] in the organization. They voted on me the other night. . . . I'd like to have the interviews in my apartment. I went to Jay's once. His roommate was there. It was so small, cluttered and cramped. John's is the same way. I just don't know if I can get them to come to my place. Jay lives all the way downtown. I mean, they're really not getting anything from me. I'm the one whose asking for the information. . . . My place is big and comfortable. Kathy's there, walking in and out. The doors are open. . . . I can't do it at [my business location], not in a car. I like things large, a lot of space.

What am I concerned about? Well, I don't have to worry about the meaning of it. I'm concerned about the sex, that they will hit on me. You know. You did research with men. They might spread rumors. . . . There was also something else. Jay told me that he put a lot of work into getting me in the organization. . . . After they passed me, he said, "I really broke my ass on this one." He said it nicely. . . . And the other thing, we had lunch, for an interview. I paid the first time, twenty dollars, because after all he's giving me the information. Then the next time, I went to pay again and he would not have it. He said we had to split it. No, he said pay alternatively. I would pay once and he'd pay the next time. . . . Well, I read that article by Marty Weinberg, he's straight isn't he? He said that there will be a time that someone will ask you to close dance and you have to make a decision about what you are going to do. If you don't expect that, then you shouldn't do the research. I haven't had to deal with that yet. I've been in groups. With Jay, I just play by the cues . . . (I congratulate the researcher about finally gaining access to the organization). Thanks. Yes. Who knew. Now I'm really gonna have to do this!

INTERVIEW 3 (SEVERAL WEEKS LATER)

Retirement's great. Yes, there's still some anxiety about it. All the free time. No, I get a permit so I can keep a gun. But, they just take all of your things away slowly, your identification, your gun, your shield. They took my shield but I have an extra. . . . It's like Goffman says. They strip you of yourself, your identity. . . . Things have been going well [in the research]. I've been interviewing this gay cop, Joe who is in the hospital. He's dying of AIDS. He has meningitis . . . Jay was supposed to meet me there but didn't show up. They're all afraid of becoming contaminated. . . . Yes I do feel more relaxed about it. I guess because I read a lot of the literature. It doesn't bother me now. I shake Joe's hand and all. I know that he is glad to talk to me. It's pretty clear that he is dying. His skin is sort of a mess. . . . [The researcher explores a dream which relates to conflicts mobilized in the research encounter.] I don't think Laud Humphreys talks at all about the kind of things that he felt when he was doing his fieldwork. He sticks in there that he was married but doesn't mention anything else. I could not do what he did. I mean he went to places and watched the men fuck and suck each other. I couldn't do that, could you? . . .

It is clear from the interviews that sexuality mediates every aspect of the researcher's first encounter with homosexual police, creating much discomfort. He does not yet understand the subjects' rules of interaction and is confused about how to interpret their communications. The environment is experienced as uncertain, sudden, and unpredictable. For example, the researcher notes several encounters with subjects in which they initially appear "straight" and, without warning, change their sexual presentation of self. At the rational level, the researcher is aware that sex is an important dimension of interaction about which a fieldworker should take note. At the same time, he is unprepared for public displays of homosexuality and views them as unwanted intrusions. By the second interview, it becomes apparent that the researcher's discomfort, initially presented in terms of a fear of getting AIDS, is partly rooted in a worry that a homosexual approach is inevitable.

At this point, it is worth reviewing the beginning of the first interview, when the researcher mentions his retirement, sinus problems, and the financial loss sustained in the stock market crash. These troubling current issues may revive old and deep insecurities. These deeper issues are likely related to the sexual concerns mobilized by the research, since they are linked associatively. For example, retirement involves a series of losses. The researcher is symbolically stripped of his identity, gives up his department-issued gun, shield, and identification card. The sinus problem is another area of perceived physical weakness and damage. The discussion about the stock market revolves around similar themes. Something valuable is taken away from the researcher. The stock market also may represent a metaphor for the fieldwork enterprise itself. At this point in time, both Wall Street and the homosexual world appear unpredictable and very risky.

By the third interview, the researcher appears relaxed about the sexual issues that previously alarmed him. He has overcome his fear of getting AIDS and is able to make hospital visits to see an organizational member who is dying of meningitis. Some concerns about homosexuality still remain. For example, it is possibly easier to get close to a dying patient than other gay subjects who are more likely to initiate a sexual relationship. Nevertheless, the researcher's comfortable interaction with the AIDS patient marks a turning point in his fieldwork which extends to relations with other subjects.

Let us review some of the defenses the researcher uses to manage the social and intrapsychic tensions experienced. When he first enters an organizational meeting, he walks in one door and out the other, a defensive parapraxis which clearly reveals his ambivalence about doing the fieldwork. At various points during the first few days in the field, the researcher expresses the wish that his wife were with him. At one level, her presence could help establish his heterosexual identity to subjects and ward off the possibility of a sexual approach. However, it is possible that her presence is also desired because it would serve to buttress his own sense of heterosexual identity in this difficult cultural setting. Ultimately, the researcher decides to arrange the first fieldwork interviews in his home because the doors are open and his wife is visible. At several points in the discussion, the researcher mentions other sociologists who conducted fieldwork among homosexuals. He assumes that they are heterosexual and thereby reassures himself regarding his own sexuality. In fact, the two sociologists mentioned are gay. The researcher's confusion regarding their sexual orientation may represent an unconscious act of denial. At this point in the research, it was possibly too problematic to acknowledge the homosexuality of other participant observers.

Denial is also used as a defense in other contexts. For example, the researcher is annoyed when a gay subject interrupts the conversation with John concerning his book. The exploration of his feeling of annoyance reveals the extent to which the sexualization of the research encounter created anxiety. Prior to the interruption by the gay policeman, the researcher was able to defend himself against his fears by claiming his interaction with John involved "business," not sex. The feeling of annoyance itself functioned to mitigate tensions as it probably increased distance between researcher and subject.

Some of the researcher's spontaneous symbolic gestures also served defensive purposes. One example is particularly notable because it involves a compromise formation which both gratifies and defends against unconscious desires. The researcher observes homosexuals at a party share drinks and becomes concerned that his will get mixed with theirs. In order to minimize the possibility of AIDS contamination, the researcher substitutes his lime cocktail for a vodka and orange juice, thereby changing the color of his drink. He tightly clutches the glass to be sure no one else will take it. He considers this latter behavior unusual and wonders if two gay psychologists will notice.

At the overt level, the orange drink gesture can be interpreted as a rational means by which the researcher managed to handle his conscious fear of getting AIDS. At an unconscious level, it is possible that more subtle dynamics are also at work. The glass the researcher holds in his hand is a breakable object. As such, it may represent the researcher's own sense of fragile phallic sexuality. He holds it tightly to protect himself from possible (symbolic) injury to his sense of masculinity and to distinguish his manhood from that of research subjects. The act of obtaining a unique drink, colored differently from others, involves an exhibition. By clutching the glass in the way described, the researcher also draws attention to himself. Through this symbolic action, the researcher allows himself to flirt with the idea that he is attractive to homosexual men. In doing so, he gratifies the conflictual wishes that are situationally mobilized in the fieldwork encounter. At the same time, however, he defends himself against the personal discomfort that would result from their being actually realized. The researcher's behavior is particularly creative as a fieldwork action because it helps manage inner tensions in a way which does not alienate research subjects.

Each defense a researcher uses to manage social and intrapsychic tensions has some role in structuring relations with subjects. In the case of this researcher, a number of effects are apparent. The fieldworker displayed intense ambivalence about doing the project when he walked in and out the door. At this point, a part of him would have welcomed an excuse not to pursue the research. At that time, the researcher was trying to get access to the organization and was involved in delicate negotiations with a psychologist member who opposed his presence. It was undoubtedly tempting to enact his ambivalence by escalating the conflict with the psychologist who might put an end to his research. As the researcher became more aware of his internal conflict, he was better able to negotiate the relationship with the psychologist. He reassured him that the focus of their books was different and agreed to put off the publication of his book for two years. As it would take at least that long to research, write, and publish the material, the contract did nothing to hurt the researcher's career and greatly facilitated friendly relations with the psychologist. Access to the organization was formally granted several weeks later.

During the interaction with John, the researcher did nothing to inhibit the development of rapport or reduce his chances to do the fieldwork. However, he was temporarily blinded to an important aspect of the relations between homosexual men. Thus, he found himself wanting to omit recognition of the sexual aspects of encounters and felt annoyed when they became sexualized. Once aware of the roots of his irritation, the sexuality became somewhat less troublesome. The researcher could then make observations about the cultural dilemmas of homosexual police without having to desexualize interactions observed.

The researcher's desire to have his wife with him during the initial phases of fieldwork was not acted upon and therefore did not substantially structure field relations. The effect of conducting the interviews at home is not clear. It is possible that it could minimize the willingness of subjects to talk about their sexual behaviors. However, the researcher makes clear that he has little curiosity about gay sexual practices and would prefer not to observe them. Detailed conversation about this subject might also arouse discomfort. Although this difficulty dealing with homosexual practices might compromise psychotherapeutic interactions or another kind of sociological study, it is unlikely to be problematic for this researcher's work.

The orange drink interaction has already been analyzed in detail. Suffice it to say that it did not appear to pose problems for research relations. Thus, the researcher was able to avoid alienating subjects by restraining from openly displaying his fear of homosexual contact. However, it is possible that the researcher's worry about contracting AIDS precluded his ability to inquire regarding how gay men themselves handled their concerns. Only later, when the researcher had worked through some of the conflicts about his own sexual status and read some literature on AIDS did he attempt to observe the way organizational members handled their fears. At this point, he noted that he was the only person to visit the police officer dying of AIDS in the hospital. Although the gay men did not seem concerned about sharing their drinks, they apparently hesitated to visit a sick colleague. By the third interview, many of the researcher's anxieties about homosexuality have abated. He has been accepted into the organization as their first heterosexual member. He feels comfortable having dinner with subjects and interviewing gay men in his home. He is also able to arrange some interviews in their apartments without undue discomfort.

This study of a heterosexual researcher doing fieldwork in a homosexual setting has explored the mediation of interactional events by unconscious transferences. It has presented the fieldwork endeavor as a process in which anxiety is routinely experienced in the face of fieldwork challenges that evoke intrapsychic conflict. Various defenses are used by the researcher to handle the social and psychological tensions, each of which structures research relations in both overt and subtle ways. The researcher who is the object of this study was able to work through many of the conflicts which were mobilized in the fieldwork encounter. As a result, defenses which enhanced distance from subjects were substituted by others which allowed more intimacy and empathy. In order to avoid testing the limits of his abilities, however, he did choose to study an aspect of the gay law enforcement organization which was least problematic. His research will focus on organizational rather than sexual politics.

Transference to the Researcher

The discussion of the psychodynamics of the fieldwork encounter has so far focused on the way the researcher's transferences inhibit relations with subjects. Brief mention has also been made of the way that researchers' transferences structure research relations in positive ways. Transferences are rarely one sided, and subjects may also project archaic images onto the person of the researcher (Crapanzano, 1980; LeVine, 1981). This is particularly likely for informants with whom the researcher develops close, long-term relationships. The cultural identity the researcher negotiates in the setting is therefore mediated by archaic roles which belong to significant others in the individual's past. The subject's transferences to the researcher are important to examine for the same reason as those of the researcher. They play a role in structuring the research relationship and the kinds of data gathered.

Sarah LeVine (1981) provides an unusually perceptive analysis of the significance of subjects' transferences for fieldwork relations. While conducting a study of childbearing among Gusii woman in southwestern Kenya, LeVine was engaged in intensive, long-term interviews with a number of woman informants. Familiar with psychoanalytic theory and method, she anticipated the likelihood that her role as foreigner and friend would become mediated by transferences.

In order to facilitate her understanding of the psychological dimensions of childbearing and help decipher the emerging transferences,

LeVine collected the dreams of informants. Dreams told in clinical and research settings not only have genetic roots but also often condense images which refer directly to the researcher. As LeVine began to develop close relations with subjects, they began to report dreams containing depictions of the researcher and her possessions. For example, LeVine's Peugeot was a prominent feature of several womens' dreams, even after it was rendered inoperative because of an accident. The significance of the Peugeot varied, depending on the particular psychodynamics of the dreamer. In one woman's dream, the car was often presented as a kind of omnipotent vehicle, capable of crossing the seas to America (LeVine, 1981, p. 286). In this transference manifestation, the researcher was apparently idealized as a strong and rational person on whose power the subject could draw in order to flee a painful personal situation, or alternatively, confront it (LeVine, 1981, p. 285).

LeVine collected the dreams of informants but was not always aware of their significance. As a result, she was not fully prepared to deal with some of the more dramatic transference reactions that emerged in the case of one informant in particular. In contrast to the other women, Sabina began to have explicit dreams about the researcher in the initial days of interviewing. Although subject to debate in psychoanalytic circles, some analysts argue that early transference dreams indicate the existence of a severe disturbance in ego functioning (e.g. Harris, 1962; Rappaport, 1959; Rosenbaum, 1965). The patient's reality testing may be impaired such that he or she cannot adequately distinguish the fantasied transference object from the real person.

LeVine understood neither the psychological implications of Sabina's communications nor the intensity of her transference. The researcher's difficulty was compounded by the development of a countertransference reaction which further inhibited understanding. As a result, the researcher was inattentive to the seriousness of certain critical events taking place in Sabina's life and blinded to the fragility of her psychological condition. Ultimately, Sabina's social situation combined with the unconscious tensions that emerged in her relationship with the researcher and resulted in the premature termination of the fieldwork encounter. LeVine explains:

> Given Sabina's labile condition at the onset of the study, she might have regressed anyway, in the face of the stresses in her life; nevertheless, I should add that my response to her may well have been a factor in promoting first her eroticized transference to me and later her precipitous

regression after the birth of her child. From the start I was fascinated by her volatility. To me, she was an exotic. I felt, indeed, that my understanding her would be something in the order of a revelation. I was also profoundly impressed by her pain. If she were seductive, I was easily seduced. In a word, I did not retain a proper distance [1981, p. 292].

LeVine concludes her study of subjects' transferences to the researcher with some important words of advice. Social scientists working in settings in which the parameters of the researcher-informant relationship are impossible to control ignore transferences at peril to the research task. It would appear that, in the event that informants report dreams in which researchers appear as themselves or thinly disguised, researchers should be cognizant of the possible significance of such material. At the very least, it indicates that the researcher has assumed unconscious as well as conscious importance in the lives of his or her informants. Researchers should also take note of their own dreams because they may provide crucial data regarding countertransferences that bear closer scrutiny. An avoidance of the task of analyzing the transferences and countertransferences which arise in the research situation may have dire consequences for the fieldwork enterprise (LeVine, 1981, p. 292). It should be noted that dreams are not the only source of information regarding the transferences which arise in the interview situation. In unstructured interviews in particular, transference references to the researcher may be thinly disguised in the informant's descriptions of other persons and experiences which bear resemblance to some aspect of the researcher or the interview setting.

Another example of the way that the transference to the researcher may structure the fieldwork data is suggested in the case of a policewoman key informant. Here, the transference appeared to provide an unconscious force which motivated the telling of a particular tale about the informal world of policing. After many months of participant observation in the Metro City Police Department, I developed a good rapport with a particular woman officer. Eventually, she told me a great deal about her occupational life, her involvements with men, her marriage, and her childhood. In fact, she was a victim of incest, her alcoholic father having molested her when she was a girl. Although it would be necessary to gather clinical data in order to determine with precision the links between her ongoing occupational life and her traumatic childhood experience, there did appear to be some relationship. For example, the policewoman allowed me to tape record a number of interviews which involved her encounters with police corruption. These narratives described her experience in terms of a series of encounters with powerful men, who, I suspect represented her father. The sexuality of these narratives is particularly poignant. In each story, a man who is supposed to be "clean," respectable, and protective, turns out to be the very person who attempts to corrupt or seduce her by trying to make her take "dirty money" or engage in extramarital sex. For example, a priest forces her to take her first "note." He pushes five dollars in her (back) pocket. She describes her reaction to the incident. "I felt dirty . . . I felt like they [other police] could read it all over my face." The captain of her precinct, who also tries to sexually seduce her, insists she make a false arrest of an innocent boy in order to appease the local political patron (Hunt and Manning, in press). The latter is jealous because the policewoman paid more attention to the dry cleaner than to him. Consequently, he tries to get her attention by having her make the arrest. Eventually, the cleaner offers to help her out of the "jam" by using his connections but then also tries to seduce her. She explains, "It was dreadful. His little beady eyes are getting all watery and he's holding my knee. . . . So when I left there I felt sick, absolutely sick. I wanted to vomit. All I could think about was all that he wanted to do for me, all he wanted was to make love to me. . . . I stood up and the next thing I know is that he's right behind me. . . ."

The officer's suggestion that money is stuffed in her "back pocket" and her worry that the "cleaner" is right behind her may represent unconscious derivatives of anal penetration and further support the hypothesis that sadomasochistic fantasies underlie her encounters with these men. The description of the cleaner as beady-eyed is also interesting. It could refer to the part of him that seemed like a "dirty old man." The metaphor is also animal-like. Psychoanalytic studies of victims of incest and child abuse suggest that their fantasies are often punctuated by multidetermined rat and mouse images (Shengold, 1967; Freud, 1909). Indeed, the woman had a mouse phobia which suggests a possible history of overstimulation.

The themes of seduction and corruption which dominate her narrative are accompanied by another, that of this officer's innocence of all wrongdoing. For example, when the captain, a powerful political patron of the mayor, and implicitly, the police commissioner, try to make her falsely arrest a black boy without probable cause, she depicts herself as the only innocent one. In contrast to the men with whom she works, the policewoman is not only willing to stand up before the Police Board of Inquiry but will also testify in court on the boy's behalf. As a whole, the "corruption tapes" provide evidence that indicts the Catholic church, the police department, and most of its male members. I suspect that her relations with these corrupt and powerful men to whom she is both attracted and repelled involved, in part, a repetition of her earlier experience with her father. She reenacts in her encounters a sadistically tinged oedipal drama.

The fact that the woman chose to be a police officer may have unconscious determinants which also relate to the incest trauma. Thus, by carrying a gun and assuming a role symbolically associated with masculinity, she minimizes her femininity and unconsciously protects herself from being the object of father-daughter incest. The defense function of a masculine identification in victims of incest has been noted in the literature (e.g. Kramer, 1983; Furman, 1956; Katan, 1973; Shengold, 1967).

The policewoman's unconscious motives for telling me these stories are probably complex. However, the roles played in her inner life would appear to have had a profound effect on the structure and content of her tale. Perhaps she found in me a witness to the crime of incest who would proclaim her innocence and her father's guilt. Thus, there was a part of her that wanted me to publish "the tapes" and expose the corruption. I was also probably a maternal transference figure who, she hoped, would protect and rescue her as her mother had not done. It is worth noting that she eventually left the police department, in part because she could no longer tolerate the corruption, the reality of which could scarcely be denied. Soon after her father died, she married a wealthy professional man who claimed to have a business relationship with the mafia. The marriage seemed to have many meanings. At one level, it may have constituted an unconscious attempt to leave the world of her father. At the same time, it possibly represented a wish to maintain a connection to him. Thus, her husband was associated with men as corrupt and powerful as the police, the priest, and her father. It is notable in this context that she never really trusted her husband to take care of her children if something happened to her. One suspects that this also related to the incest trauma.

5. CONCLUSIONS

The sociological literature on fieldwork focuses on the interactional dimensions of the fieldwork encounter. Researcher-subject relations are examined in terms of the roles researchers play in the field and their effect on data gathering. In contrast to classical researchers, existentialists recognize that researcher subjectivity has positive as well as negative implications for research relations and data gathering. They acknowledge that fieldwork is far less rational than depicted in classical accounts. The link between the researcher's cultural roles and feeling states is important to examine because it helps structure relations with subjects, the data gathered, and the construction of the sociological narrative. While existentalist researchers recognize that researcher subjectivity is important in fieldwork, they omit consideration of its intrapsychic dimensions.

This essay attempts to go beyond both classical and existential accounts to explore the implications of a psychoanalytic point of view for the relations between researcher, subject, and data gathered. It does not challenge either existential or hermeneutic methodologies. In contrast, it shares the view that a dualism between subject and object is problematic because fieldwork is an intersubjective process. It is also interpretive, mediated by the minds of both researcher and subjects. However, the psychoanalytic perspective adds an additional dimension to the sociological understanding of fieldwork, which provides richness and depth. Fieldwork does not only involve a process in which the researcher negotiates social roles and cultural symbols. It also is a dialogue which is mediated by complex intrapsychic meanings of researcher and subjects. The inner worlds of researchers structure their choice of setting, experience in the initial stages of fieldwork, and the research roles they assume. The transferences that are situationally mobilized in the fieldwork encounter have implications for the questions researchers ask, the answers they hear, and the materials they observe. Most important, transferences structure the researcher's ability to develop empathic relations with those subjects who provide the essential source of sociological data. Subjects also develop transferences to researchers, which may have a profound effect on the stories they tell to researchers and their relations with them.

Few psychoanalytic studies of the fieldwork endeavor are published in the social science literature. While some anthropologists have made major contributions in the area of psychoanalysis and fieldwork, sociologists remain skeptical and have not attempted to explore the implications of psychoanalytic theory and method for the research endeavor. This is not to say that psychoanalysis is completely foreign to contemporary sociology. In contrast, it has been incorporated into recent studies within some subdisciplines, in particular gender roles. However, most works dismiss the contributions of Freud and focus instead on preoedipal object relations. As a result, they also omit consideration of intrapsychic conflict and the rich world of unconscious meanings which mediate everyday life. Even ethnomethodologists who study the invisible world of the taken for granted have omitted consideration of its deeper significance.

Sociological skepticism about psychoanalysis has structured the materials that researchers have made available for scholars attempting to study the unconscious dimensions of everyday life. In terms of the study of fieldwork, for example, most researchers have not collected the kinds of data that would facilitate an in-depth psychoanalytic study. As a result, this monograph is limited in parts and necessarily speculative in others. However, it is my hope that it will help sociologists develop a more sophisticated understanding of psychoanalysis and inspire other fieldworkers to devise ways to examine a domain of research relations that has hitherto remained hidden.

Researchers currently doing fieldwork can begin this exploration by routinely collecting new sorts of data. Dreams, fantasies, jokes, and parapraxes, for example, are some kinds of data that provide access to unconscious processes. Researchers' own emotional responses to particular encounters also may add knowledge regarding their possible transference reactions. Researchers who endeavor to collect data about the unconscious dimension of everyday life should be explicit in fieldnotes about the situational context in which the relevant phenomena appear. If possible, they should record their associations to these materials in much the same way as Freud (1900) in *The Interpretation of Dreams*.

The very process of gathering these kinds of data will facilitate another aspect of the psychoanalytic study of fieldwork and culture. Thus, researchers' attunement to their own inner lives may facilitate some working through of transference reactions that are interfering with empathic communication with research subjects. It also may help overcome resistances to collecting new materials about the subjects' world which could open up innovative ways of understanding the relationship between culture and unconscious. Inquiry into the dreams, fantasies, and finely tuned affective states of research subjects could add much to our understanding of the psychocultural construction of meaning worlds. Conducting unstructured, "free associative" interviews following stressful events, including exposure to injury and death, would be a particularly useful means to gather data regarding the deep structure of subjects' reactions. From this material, generalizations could be made regarding both the cultural and intrapsychic issues that are mobilized in the face of such events, which would further enlighten scholars to hitherto unexplored dimensions of occupational behavior.

Despite my own conviction that the informed application of psychoanalytic theory and method to the study of the social world can lead to rich new discoveries, there are some difficulties in the enterprise which should be kept in mind. Few sociologists are familiar with psychoanalytic thinking. Most have not had clinical experience or the benefit of a personal analysis. They often are only superficially acquainted with the works of Freud and unaware of the current literature in classical psychoanalysis. It is difficult for analysts themselves to persist in the arduous task of self-analysis, even with formal courses in theory and method, years of experience with patients, and a personal training analysis. The problems for sociologists attempting to do applied psychoanalysis may therefore seem formidable.

Ideally, sociologists could facilitate the psychoanalytic study of fieldwork methods and culture by obtaining formal training and/or a personal analysis. The benefit of formal training and/or a personal analysis is reflected in the works of many prominent researchers on psychoanalytic topics, including Steven Marcus (1984), Peter Gay (1988), Janet Malcolm (1983), and Waud Kracke (1978). However, a personal analysis is hardly practical for most sociologists in view of its costliness and the amount of time involved. Sociologists who seek formal training in classical psychoanalysis will also encounter a number of difficulties related to the negotiation of full-time academic and clinical careers. Beyond the organizational, financial, and practical problems of developing a sufficient understanding of psychoanalysis, there are also issues of researcher personality. The sociological fieldworker is typically an action-oriented person. The ability to simultaneously be introspective and interactive during the research encounter is full of complex social and personal contradictions (Kracke, 1987b). Attunement to both inner and outer worlds of research subjects is also a difficult task.

In view of the many complexities of doing applied psychoanalysis, researchers will inevitably make mistakes and be tempted to indulge in "wild analysis." In contrast to the clinician, fieldworkers do not have the benefit of psychoanalyzing their subjects to see if their hypotheses about their inner lives bear out in long-term treatment. They therefore hazard reading too much into surface derivatives, imposing their own fantasies onto the data or psychologizing culture. One way unanalyzed researchers can temper their imagination to best fit the data is by checking explorations with subjects, if that possibility arises. Researchers may also share their findings with colleagues formally trained in psychoanalytic theory and method who could provide useful comments.

It should be noted that psychoanalysis involves the exploration of aspects of individuals' inner lives that are both delicate and deeply personal. The researcher must remain both empathetically and ethically attuned to any persons who are the object of investigation to ensure the privacy of their communications. On some occasions, important data must be disguised or omitted, just as it is in traditional fieldwork studies. Despite the difficulties of doing applied psychoanalysis, its creative possibilities are large. If I have not proved my case for scientifically minded sociologists, I hope that I have at least sparked their curiosity about the application of psychoanalytic theory and method to the study of fieldwork and social life.

NOTES

1. The oedipus complex refers to a constellation of fantasies about parents of both sexes which boys and girls usually experience between the ages of three to six. As part of the "negative oedipal" constellation, the boy identifies with the feminine role and takes his father as the love object. With "positive oedipal" feelings, the reverse occurs, and the mother is the object of the boy's desire. The wishes involved in positive oedipal fantasies present a conflict for the boy because he loves and admires his father at the same time that he is jealous of him. The boy also fears that he will be punished for his aggressive fantasies. In order to avoid castration, he may regress to phase-specific fantasies which seem less hazardous. For example, negative oedipal wishes towards his father may dominate his thoughts. These regressive fantasies contain their own inner dilemmas and push the boy forward once again. For example, an identification with his mother, evident in the negative oedipal solution, also involves symbolic castration. Typically, boys resolve these complex issues by putting off the fulfillment of their sexual desires until they are older and can have a woman of their own. At the same time, they identify with the father and thereby reduce their competition with him. The oedipal complex in girls is similar to that of boys. However, the girl's desire to have her mother as a sexual object is associated with negative oedipal thoughts. Her desire to displace her mother and have her father's love is part of the positive oedipal constellation. It should be noted that the development of gender identity and sexuality is complex, and there are other resolutions of the oedipal scenario besides the development of heterosexuality and a primary identification with the same sex parent.

2. Although I did not consciously connect the two incidents at the time they occurred, I subsequently recalled an earlier incident in which a man had killed his girlfriend by putting a rifle in her vagina and pulling the trigger.

3. An encounter with the attending psychopharmacologist was particularly disturbing. Thinking he was a resident, I politely introduced myself and inquired if I could accompany him on interviews of patients. He responded by rudely interrogating me about my right to be there and then ejecting me from the E.R. This was done in front of the very residents whom I was trying to befriend.

4. There are a number of possible meanings of the medical degree which vary with the psychodynamics of each psychiatrist. The medical degree may assume superiority in the unconscious mental life of some individuals by virtue of its symbolic association with the phallus. Some psychiatrists display both phallic narcissism and castration anxiety by indirectly designating some segment of the population as inferior. For other physicians, the question of phallic-oedipal rivalry may be salient. Thus, the Ph.D. opponent becomes the symbolic victim of castration. The medical doctor's fears that he is castrated, weak, homosexual, passive, and simply "not sharp enough" to do the job, are projected onto the Ph.D. Finally, psychiatry is a degraded occupation in medicine. Psychiatrists may, therefore, be involved in an identification with the aggressor when they treat psycholo-

gists in a similar manner as they have been treated by physicians who claim superior organizational status. It should be noted that most psychiatrists who become analysts are psychoanalyzed by medical doctor training analysts who, themselves, may not have fully explored the unconscious meanings of the medical degree. As a result, an intrapsychic blindspot is reproduced in each generation of analysts. It is also reinforced socially by the hierarchical structure of the American medical establishment.

5. In recent years, a number of psychoanalytic studies have been published which examine the importance of surrogate mothers in the lives of children and adults (Hardin 1988a, 1988b). Freud himself had a maid who had a profound impact on his life and even his practice of psychoanalysis. The maid, Nora, was fired when Freud was two and one half years old because she had stolen family property. Her sudden departure had a traumatic effect on the boy (Hardin, 1988a, 1988b; Glenn, 1986). Freud's patient Dora was apparently the victim of a surrogate maternal countertransference. Dora gave Freud a fortnight's warning of her impending departure, the typical time provided by domestic servants who are about to leave their household of work. Her abrupt leaving apparently mobilized feelings surrounding his abandonment by his maid. Freud became angry at Dora and expressed this in his childish reaction to her departure as well as his refusal to take her back into treatment when she asked for his help some time later (Glenn, 1986).

REFERENCES

Adler, P. A. and P. Adler (1987) Membership Roles in Field Research. Beverly Hills, CA: Sage.

Adler, P. A. (1985) Wheeling and Dealing: An Ethnography of an Upper-Level Drug Dealing and Smuggling Community. New York: Columbia University.

Agar, M. (1980a) The Professional Stranger: An Informal Introduction to Ethnography. New York: Academic Press.

Agar, M. (1980b) "Hermeneutics in anthropology: a review essay." Ethos 8: 253-271.

Anderson, B. G. (1971) "Adaptive aspects of culture shock." American Anthropologist 73: 1121-1125.

Bittner, E. (1980) The Functions of the Police in Modern Society. Cambridge, MA: Oelgeschlager, Gunn, and Hain.

Blum, H. P. (1977) Female Psychology: Contemporary Psychoanalytic Views. New York: International Universities Press.

Blum, H. P. (1986) "Countertransference and the theory of technique: A discussion." Journal of the American Psychoanalytic Association 34: 309-329.

Bohannon, L. (1954) Return to Laughter. New York: Harper and Row.

Boyer, B. L. (1979) Childhood and Folklore: A Psychoanalytic Study of Apache Personality. New York: The Library of Psychological Anthropology.

Briggs, J. L. (1970) Never in Anger: Portrait of an Eskimo Family. Cambridge, MA: Harvard University Press.

Briggs, J. L. (1987) "In search of emotional meaning." Ethos 15: 8-16.

Caudill, W. (1961) "Some problems of transnational communication: Japan-U.S. The application of psychiatric insight to cross-cultural communication." Group for the Advancement of Psychiatry Symposium (No 7): 409-421.

Cesara, M. (1982) Reflections of a Woman Anthropologist: No Hiding Place. New York: Academic Press.

Chagnon, N. A. (1974) Studying the Yanomamo. New York: Holt, Rinehart and Winston.

Chagnon, N. A. (1968) Yanomamo: The Fierce People. New York: Holt, Rinehart and Winston.

Clark, C. (1987) "Sympathy biography and sympathy margin." American Journal of Sociology 93: 290-321.

Crapanzano, V. (1980) Tuhami: A Portrait of a Moroccan. Chicago: University of Chicago Press.

Denzin, N. K. (1970) The Research Act: A Theoretical Introduction to Sociological Methods. Berkeley: University of California Press.

Devereux, G. (1967) From Anxiety to Method in the Behavioral Sciences. The Hague, Netherlands: Mouton.

Douglas, J. D. (1976) Investigative Social Research. Beverly Hills, CA: Sage.

Douglas, J. D. (1985) Creative Interviewing. Beverly Hills, CA: Sage.

88

Douglas, J. D. and J. M. Johnson (eds.) (1977) Existential Sociology. Cambridge, MA: Cambridge University Press.

Edelson, M. (1984) Hypothesis and Evidence in Psychoanalysis. Chicago: University of Chicago Press.

Esman, A. H. (1987) "Rescue fantasies." The Psychoanalytic Quarterly LVI: 263-271.

Freeman, D. (1983) Margaret Mead in Samoa: The Making and Unmaking of an Anthropological Myth. Cambridge, MA: Harvard University Press.

Freilich, M. (1970) Marginal Natives: Anthropologists at Work. New York: Harper and Row.

Freud, S. (1900) "The interpretation of dreams." Standard Edition 1.

Freud, S. (1901) "The psychopathology of everyday life." Standard Edition 6.

Freud, S. (1909a) "Notes upon a case of obsessional neurosis." Standard Edition 10: 55-318.

Freud, S. (1910) "A special type of choice of object made by men." Standard Edition 11: 163-177.

Freud, S. (1920) "The psychogenesis of a case of homosexuality in a woman." Standard Edition 18: 145-175.

Freud, S. (1922) "Medusa's head." Standard Edition 18: 273-274.

Furman, E. (1956) "An ego disturbance in a young child." Psychoanalystic Study of the Child 1: 312-355.

Gans, H. J. (1968) "The participant-observer as a human being: Observations on the personal aspects of field work," pp. 300-317 in H. S. Becker, B. Greer, D. Riesman and R. S. Weiss (eds.) Institutions and the Person. Chicago: Aldine.

Garza-Guerrera, A. C. (1974) "Culture shock: Its mourning and the vicissitudes of identity." Journal of the American Psychoanalytic Association 22: 408-429.

Gay, P. (1988) Freud: A Life for Our Time. New York: W. W. Norton.

Glenn, J. (1984) "Psychic trauma and masochism." Journal of the American Psychoanalytic Association 32: 357-385.

Glenn, J. (1986) "Freud, Dora and the maid: a study of countertransference." Journal of the American Psychoanalytic Association 34: 591-607.

Gregor, T. (1985) Anxious Pleasures: The Sexual Life of Amazonian People. Chicago: University of Chicago Press.

Grossman, W. I. and W. A. Stewart (1977) "Penis envy: from childhood wish to developmental metaphor," pp. 193-213 in H. Blum (ed.) Female Psychology: Contemporary Psychoanalytic Views. New York: International Universities Press.

Gurney, J. N. (1985) "Not one of the guys: The female researcher in a male-dominated setting." Qualitative Sociology 8: 42-61.

Hardin, H. T. (1988a) "On the vicissitudes of Freud's early mothering I: Early environment and loss." The Psychoanalytic Quarterly LVI: 628-645.

Hardin, H. T. (1988b) "On the vicissitudes of Freud's early mothering II: Alienation from his biological mother." The Psychoanalytic Quarterly LVII: 72-87.

Harris, I. (1962) "Dreams about the analyst." International Journal of Psychoanalysis 43: 151-158.

Hayano, David M. (1982) Poker Faces: The Life and Work of Professional Card Players. Berkeley: University of California Press.

Heimann, P. (1950) "On countertransference" International Journal of Psychoanalysis 31: 81-84.

Hochschild, A. R. (1983) The Managed Heart: The Commercialization of Human Feeling. Berkeley: University of California Press.

Hook, S. (1960) Psychoanalysis, Scientific Method and Philosophy. New York: Grove Press.

Horowitz, R. (1986) "Remaining an outsider: Membership as a threat to research rapport." Urban Life 14: 409-431.

Hughes, E. C. (1971) The Sociological Eye. Chicago: Aldine.

Humphreys, L. (1970) Tearoom Trade: Impersonal Sex in Public Places. Chicago: Aldine.

Hunt, J. C. (1987) "Review of women guarding men, by Lynn E. Zimmer." Work and Occupations 14: 471-473.

Hunt, J. C. (1984) "The development of rapport through the negotiation of gender in field work among police." Human Organization 43: 283-296.

Hunt, J. C. (1985) "Police accounts of normal force." Urban Life 13: 315-341.

Hunt, J. C. (in press) "The logic of sexism among police" Women & Criminal Justice.

Hunt, J. C. and P. K. Manning (in press) "The social context of police lying," in Peter K. Manning and John Van Maanen (eds.) Policing: A View From the Street, 2nd edition. New York: Aldine.

Hunt, J. C. and M. Rudden. (1986) "Gender differences in the psychology of parenting: Psychoanalytic and feminist perspectives." Journal of the American Academy of Psychoanalysis 14: 213-225.

Jacobs, T. J. (1983) "The analyst and the patient's object world: Notes on an aspect of countertransference." Journal of the American Psychoanalytic Association 13: 38-56.

Jacobs, T. J. (1886) "On countertransference enactments." Journal of the American Psychoanalytic Association 34: 289-309.

Johnson, J. M. (1975) Doing Field Research. New York: Free Press.

Jones, E. (1961) The Life and Work of Sigmund Freud. New York: Basic Books.

Junker, B. H. (1960) Field Work: An Introduction to the Social Sciences. New York: Humanities Press.

Katan, A. (1973) "Children who were raped." Psychoanalytic Study of the Child 28: 208-224.

Kern, R. (1978) "Countertransference and spontaneous screens: An analyst studies his own visual images." Journal of the American Psychoanalytic Association 26: 21-47.

Kilborne, B. J. (1981) "Moroccan dream interpretation and culturally constituted defense mechanisms." Ethos 9: 294-312.

Kracke, W. (1987a) "Encounter with other cultures: Psychological and epistemological aspects." Ethos 15: 58-82.

Kracke, W. (1987b) "A psychoanalyst in the field: Erikson's contributions to anthropology," pp. 35-70 in J. Rabow, G. M. Platt and M. Goldman (eds.) Advances in Psychoanalytic Sociology. Malabar, FL: Robert E. Krieger Publishing Company.

Kracke W. (1978) Force and Persuasion: Leadership in an Amazonia Society. Chicago: University of Chicago Press.

Kracke, W. (1985) Encounter with Other Cultures: Psychological and Epistemological Aspects: Prepublished copy of manuscript.

Kramer, S. (1983) "Object-coercive doubting: A pathological defensive response to maternal incest." Journal of the American Psychoanalytic Association 31: 325-351.

LeVine, R. A. (1982) Culture, Behavior and Personality. New York: Aldine.

LeVine, S. (1981) "Dreams of the informant about the researcher: Some difficulties inherent in the research relationships." Ethos 9: 276-294.

Lewis, O. (1963) Life in a Mexican Village: Tepoztlan Restudied. Champaign: University of Illinois Press.

Lifton, R. J. (1986) The Nazi Doctors: Medical Killing and the Psychology of Genocide. New York: Basic Books.

Little, M. (1951) "Countertransference and the patient's response to it." International Journal of Psychoanalysis 32: 32-40.

Lofland, J. (1971) Analyzing Social Settings. Belmont, CA: Wadsworth.

Malcolm, J. (1983) In the Freud Archives. New York: Random House.

Malinowski, B. (1967) A Diary in the Strict Sense of the Word. New York: Harcourt, Brace and World.

Manning, P. K. (1987) Semiotics and Fieldwork. Beverly Hills, CA: Sage.

Manning, P. K. (1972) "Observing the police: Deviants, respectables and the law," in J. Douglas (ed.) Research on Deviance. New York: Random House.

Manning, P. K. (1980) "Violence and the police role." Annals AAPSS 452: 135-144.

Marcus, S. (1984) Freud and the Culture of Psychoanalysis. New York: W. W. Norton.

Martin, S. (1980) Breaking and Entering: Policewoman on Patrol. Berkeley: University of California Press.

Maybury-Lewis, D. (1965) The Savage and the Innocent. London: Evans.

Mead, M. (1923) Coming of Age in Samoa. New York: William Morrow.

Mehan, H. and H. Wood. (1975) The Reality of Ethnomethodology. New York: John Wiley.

Miller, S. M. (1952) "The participant observer and 'over-rapport.' " American Sociological Review 17: 97-99.

Mitchell, J. (1974) Psychoanalysis and Feminism. New York: Vintage.

Obeyesekere, G. (1981) Medusa's Hair: An Essay on Personal Symbols and Religious Experience. Chicago: University of Chicago Press.

Park, R. (1915) "The city: Suggestions for the investigation of human behavior in the urban environment." American Journal of Sociology 20: 577-612. Glencoe, IL: Free Press.

Pollner, M. and R. M. Emerson. (1983) "The dynamics of inclusion and distance in fieldwork relations," pp. 235-252 in R. M. Emerson (ed.) Contemporary Field Research. Boston: Little, Brown.

Punch, M. (1986) The Politics and Ethics of Fieldwork. Beverly Hills, CA: Sage.

Punch, M. (1978) "Backstage: Observing police work in Amsterdam." Urban Life 7: 309-335.

Rabinow, P. (1977) Reflections on Fieldwork in Morocco. Berkeley: University of California Press.

Rappaport, T. (1959) "The first dream in an eroticized transference." International Journal of Psychoanalysis 40: 291-296.

Redfield, R. (1973) Tepoztlan, a Mexican Village: A Study of Folk Life. Chicago: University of Chicago Press.

Reinharz, S. (1984) On Becoming A Social Scientist. New Brunswick, NJ: Transaction Books.

Ricoeur, P. (1970) Freud and Philosophy: An Essay on Interpretation. New Haven, CT: Yale University Press.

Riesman, P. (1974) Freedom in Fulani Social Life. Chicago: University of Chicago Press.

Robbins, T., D. Anthony and T. E. Curtis. (1973) "The limits of symbolic realism: Problems of empathic observation in a sectarian context." Journal for the Scientific Study of Religion 12: 259-271.

Rosenbaum, M. (1965) "Dreams in which the analyst appears undisguised: A statistical study." Psychoanalytic Quarterly 34: 97-107.

Rubinstein, J. (1973) City Police. New York: Farrar, Strauss & Giroux.

Schatzman, L. and A. L. Strauss. (1973) Field Research: Strategies for a Natural Sociology. Englewood Cliffs, NJ: Prentice-Hall.

Schwartz, M. S., and C. G. Schwartz. (1955) "Problems in participant observation." American Journal of Sociology 60: 343-354.

Searles, H. (1970) Countertransference and Related Subjects. New York: International Universities Press.

Shaffir, W. B., R. A. Stebbins, and A. Turowetz. (1980) Fieldwork Experience: Qualitative Approaches to Social Research. New York: St. Martin's Press.

Shengold, L. (1967) "The effects of overstimulation: Rat people." International Journal of Psychoanalysis 48: 403-415.

Shengold, L. (1980) "More on rats and rat people," pp. 181-202 in M. Kanzer and J. Glenn (eds.) Freud and His Patients. New York: Jason Aronson.

Silverman, M. (1985) "Countertransference and the myth of the perfectly analyzed analyst." Psychoanalytic Quarterly 54: 175-199.

Stoller, R. J. (1985) Presentations of Gender. New Haven, CT: Yale University Press.

Sudnow, D. (1978) Ways of the Hand. New York: Harper and Row.

Thompson, H. (1967) Hell's Angels. Harmondsworth: Penguin.

Van Maanen, J. (1988) Tales of the Field. Chicago: University of Chicago Press.

Van Maanen, J. (1982) "Fieldwork on the beat," pp. 103-152 in J. Van Maanen, J. M. Dabbs, and R. R. Faulkner (eds.) Varieties of Qualitative Research. Beverly Hills, CA: Sage.

Van Maanen, J. (1978) "Epilogue: On watching the watchers," pp. 292-308 in P. K. Manning and J. Van Maanen (eds.) Policing: A View from the Street. Santa Monica, CA: Goodyear.

Wax, R. (1971) Doing Fieldwork: Warnings and Advice. Chicago: University of Chicago Press.

Wax, R. (1983) "The ambiguities of fieldwork," pp. 191-203 in R. Emerson (ed.) Contemporary Field Research. Boston: Little, Brown.

Webb, E. J., D. T. Campbell, R. D. Schwartz, and L. Sechrest (1966) Unobtrusive Measures: Nonreactive Research in the Social Sciences. Chicago: Rand McNally.

Wengle, J. L. (1984) "Anthropological training and the quest for immortality." Ethos 12: 223-244.

Whyte, W. F. (1955) Street Corner Society. Chicago: University of Chicago Press.

Winnicott, D. (1949) "Hate in the countertransference." International Journal of Psychoanalysis 30: 69-75.

Zimmer, L. (1986) Women Guarding Men. Chicago: University of Chicago Press.

ABOUT THE AUTHOR

JENNIFER C. HUNT is Associate Professor of Sociology at Montclair State College and a Research Candidate in the full clinical training program of the Psychoanalytic Institute, Department of Psychiatry, New York University Medical Center. Her research interests include medical sociology, the sociology of police, gender roles, qualitative research methods, and psychoanalysis. She is particularly concerned with applying psychoanalytic theory and method to the exploration of cultural phenomena and is initiating a study of the social and intrapsychic dimensions of physician socialization.

NOTES

NOTES